TAXI SCIENCE

THE PSYCHOLOGY OF CONSCIENCE AWAKENING

Andrew Njanjo

Matador
Unit E2 Airfield Business Park,
Harrison Road, Market Harborough,
Leicestershire. LE16 7UL
Tel: 0116 2792299
Email: books@troubador.co.uk
Web: www.troubador.co.uk/matador
Twitter: @matadorbooks

ISBN 978 1803131 139

British Library Cataloguing in Publication Data.
A catalogue record for this book is available from the British Library.

Printed and bound by CPI Group (UK) Ltd, Croydon, CR0 4YY
Typeset in 11pt Minion Pro by Troubador Publishing Ltd, Leicester, UK

Matador is an imprint of Troubador Publishing Ltd

I dedicate this book to my children, who will never have experienced my struggle. They have given me my character and are the reason I have become the hardworking person I am today. By recounting my journey in this book, my experience will be documented for them to read.

"Whatever political and social position we're holding, it is affecting someone negatively. Understanding the struggle of others can be the beginning of creating a better world but it can only happen if we're truthful to our consciousness. Each chapter in my book serves as a mirror to the behaviour we hold emotionally dear."

CONTENTS

ONE

B ecoming a taxi driver was a way to escape from the tribalism I had since from my childhood in Cameroon. I also used it as a shield for the racism I encountered upon arriving in London. The metallic protection of a cab, together with the engine of ten horsepower to get away, became my safeguard. It put me in a commanding position and in charge of my working environment. I also have the freedom to choose my working times. The two cultures that I've had the privilege to live under became my focus point that dictated my decisions throughout my twenty-five years of taxi driving. Every rider I have ever had the privilege to carry in my taxicab had a story and have always left me with a lifetime experience. I have become a behaviour therapist because of the challenging information they have left me with. I love people from every walk of life because they make a colourful, antagonistic, and stressful but wonderful world. From my experiences, I have come to understand that judging people before I have the chance to know them has never and will never be a good idea. I have been wrong about some riders who I have had the greatest and most enjoyable experiences with when I carried them in my cab for the first time. I have also been deceived by some riders whom I trusted naïvely and, yes, I got it completely wrong. Making a living from the frontline is not simply black or white, there are lots of grey moments too. However, my marriage to both my inherent cultures gave me a unique approach to the challenge. I have reached a point where I'm reactive rather than proactive because thinking that the next rider will have a similar behaviour to the previous rider is bigger than a mistake. From my experience, it's even criminal to pre-empt a rider because I could be giving the image of a criminal to a law-abiding citizen.

I have come to understand that a rider's behaviour is dictated by their subconscious mind based on their worst taxi experience. If they have previously been molested by a criminal cab driver, they will react to this experience. During a winter period, around 6 p.m., I took a female rider on a trip to Beckenham. I used a direct route through Dulwich Village and also used the private road. It was an unusual route because most drivers avoided that road due to the toll-gate there. My rider was sitting directly behind me and I noticed when I was crossing the quiet area that she moved to the middle seat. Through the rear-view mirror, I noticed she was looking nervously at both sides of the road.

'Are we going to Beckenham?' she asked.

'Yes ma'am, we are,' I replied.

In a nervous voice, she said, 'I've never been through this way before.'

'It's a private road that cuts out the traffic jam on the south circular,' I replied.

I reached the long stretch at Crystal Palace Park Road in no time.

'Oh! I know where I am now,' she said.

It would've been a big mistake on my part if I'd responded negatively about why she was questioning my choice of route. It was the first time that I was driving her and probably the last time. She had no knowledge of my background and I knew nothing about her past experience. My rider's behaviour proved one thing for sure, I knew she wasn't from that part of London. As a taxi driver, I am sometimes anxious when I'm on trips with riders I'm not familiar with but I'm good at disguising my fear. The nature of driving people in a taxicab comes with more risk than other forms of transport. Even though riders may request a taxi, or hail one, the drivers always get a stranger in the cab. Trust is the only reliable initiative both the driver and the rider have to complete a trip. The paying rider hopes that the authority has vetted the driver as a trusted and fit person to drive strangers. We are ever surrounded by danger but unconsciously believe that bad things only happened to others.

London is a unique capital city which accommodates every nationality. People live closely and on top of each other, and that is a challenge. The complexity of London's narrow and complicated roads gives room for two types of taxi. The public hire, famously known as black cabs, and the private hire also known as mini-cabs. Both provide the service of transporting riders for a commercial purpose. The black cab uses a unique designated vehicle which segregates the rider from the driver with a transparent plastic shield. There is no front seat for a rider. Black cab drivers know London's streets very well at a nine-miles radius from the centre point. The black cab is arguably one of the best taxi services in the world. They are allowed to charge by the time spent in the taxi rather than the distance. With London traffic, it's too expensive to hire a black cab. The drivers are high earners in the taxi trade and for that reason I was tempted to do The Knowledge and become a black cab driver. I did register and attended the initial induction, but the examiner said something which made me review my position.

'Maybe two or three of you in this room will actually pass the knowledge,' the examiner told us.

There were twenty-five of us in the room.

'Most of you will start the process but will give up halfway. And it's a waste of your time if you're not mentally prepared or capable,' the examiner continued.

It was like he was talking directly to me. I was only focused on the benefits of becoming a black cab driver. But I was only focused on the financial benefits of becoming a black cab driver, ignoring the hard work needed to acquire the knowledge of London.

'You should all go home and think carefully … make a decision one way or the other,' he concluded.

At home I was struggling to help my daughter with her homework. The little education that I had had while growing up in Cameroon was in French. Before I brought my daughter to the United Kingdom, I was having a conversation with some top civil servants in Cameroon. They knew I was from London, and asked me what my profession there was. When I told them I was a taxi driver, they were speechless and the subject was changed. People considered the taxi driving profession as low in the

DRIVING INTO ENLIGHTENMENT

professional rankings, even though I was financially better off than those guys. They may have been more educated than me because they had parents who sponsored them. Education is not free at every level in Cameroon. The only thing a parent can never buy for their children, whatever their wealth, is intelligence. I may not have their level of education but my intellectual capacity is unquestionable. When I got home that day, I reflected on my entire life and asked myself if I was at the end of my journey. I decided that I had a lot more to offer than driving a taxi all my life. However, if I'd known I would be doing the same job for twenty-five years, I would have taken a different decision. Nevertheless, I've benefited greatly by driving strangers with real social and political experience.

Becoming a mini-cab driver after I passed my driving test was a dream. I bought my first car and got it insured to use as private hire. At the time, it was all I needed to begin earning in my long-term dream career. When I started driving, I did not know I was beginning one of the most knowledgeable experiences of my life while earning a living. I came to London as a young adult; therefore, my viewpoint was always different from a born and bred Londoner. My background has always informed the way I have analysed the experiences acquired during exchanges with my riders. I was born in Cameroon. When I tell people where I'm from, most of them remember it for the great football team. The most memorable has always been the 1990 World Cup tournament hosted by Italy. Roger Miller, the famous dancing centre-forward, and recently, the best striker the world have ever seen, Samuel Eto'o, are the two most popular people in Cameroon. When I was growing up, there was no national television until 1987 before Cameroon television (CTV) was founded. The corporation's biggest investment was to secure the right to broadcast the American television series *Dynasty* and *Dallas*. They were very big at the time and most people, including myself, enjoyed them. Television series that reflected nothing, enjoyed by ninety-five percent of people in Europe. When I started planning my move to London, my vision was confused in believing that I was going to have the lifestyle enjoyed by the oil-rich family. Arriving in London with a primary goal of obtaining a British driving licence, I did many small jobs to raise sufficient money to access a driving school. Most of my jobs were cleaning, and washing up in the kitchen as a porter. So, after passing my driving test at Hither Green in 1996, I decided to embark on a new career. I abandoned my job of porter in the kitchen of King's College Hospital and another cleaning job I was doing alongside it. Walworth Road, London SE17 was where I began driving a mini-cab. Little did I know that I was going to be doing my job in some of the most dangerous estates in Europe. Aylesbury Estate, Heygate Estate and Peckham Park Estate, famously known as the neighbourhood of Manchester United and England's centre-back Rio Ferdinand. There were no other areas with more violence and criminal activity in London than our cab office pick-up zone.

Private-hire drivers are proportionally the majority in the taxi trade. There were immigration problems in the trade, since a large proportion of the drivers are migrants or descendants of. There was regular information about illegal migrants working as mini-cab drivers. That information was just more salt in the wound for the mini-cab trade. My accent and image made the perfect E-fit of a suspected illegal immigrant. The main insult angry riders used was to insult me as an illegal immigrant. It wasn't just from riders, it happened around the cab office too where parking spaces were limited. Many neighbours could not find a parking space because mini-cab drivers had parked and occupied the free spaces while waiting for the next trip. Our cab office was situated at Westmorland Road which was full of business premises and residential accommodations. This created resentment towards us and, after a parking space dispute, one businesswoman insulted me for being an illegal immigrant. The woman had a preferred space near her shop where she liked to park. If a cab was parked there, she would often politely ask the driver to move so she could park there. However, one day when I was parked there, I didn't receive the same respectful demands as my white colleagues received.

'Hey! Remove your cab from there. That's my space,' she shouted at me from her car.

I didn't acknowledge her demands. After about five minutes of waiting for me to move, she drove into another space. She walked back towards me.

'Why are you behaving like you're deaf? You're not allowed to park there,' she told me.

'There's no reserved parking space on this street,' I replied.

She pointed at her shop.

'This is my shop. I pay business rates and council tax here. Therefore, this space belongs to me,' she told me.

'I'm parked on the road and I pay road tax, like any other road user. I'm allowed to park here,' I replied.

She looked at me in a disgusting manner.

'Stupid fool,' she insulted me. 'I'll get my son to deal with you … illegal immigrant.'

I laughed sarcastically. The woman was African herself and not born in the UK, just like me, judging from her accent. My white colleagues witnessed the scene.

'How do you know he's an illegal immigrant?' one asked.

'Just by looking at him,' she said. 'He is an illegal immigrant, and is definitely driving a mini-cab illegally.'

My colleague drivers did not question the business neighbour in regard to the wrongful allegation, but to be spiteful to me. The woman didn't even know my name but she was certain I was an illegal immigrant and illegally driving a mini-cab. I have never been illegally resident in the UK. Despite that, I was determined that nothing could stop me achieving my goal of making a living behind the wheel of my cab. I had worked hard to obtain a UK driving licence just to become a mini-cab driver. As long as I knew I was not an illegal immigrant and I was not illegally driving a taxicab, I was good to go.

Private-hire drivers were also wrongly accused of receiving social benefits while earning. The cash-in-hand nature of the job facilitated those who had the intention to break the law. None of the private-hire operators required a driver's national insurance number. Her Majesty's Revenue and Customs (HMRC) could not verify if a claimant was making money from private-hire activity. However, not every private-hire driver was using that loophole, including myself. I have never claimed Jobseeker's Allowance in the UK but it was one of the main insults I received. I was given a trip at Kennington Job Centre after a white driver returned from the job as a no show for an unexplained reason. When

I arrived at the pick-up address, the rider was waiting. She was wary of being late for her appointment.

'I've been waiting outside my office for over thirty minutes,' she told me. 'Why're you so late?' 'I have just received the job,' I replied.

I drove as quickly as I could to get her to her appointment. When I got back to the cab office, I told the driver who had returned from the job that the rider had been waiting outside her office.

'She was the caseworker I signed on with earlier,' he told me.

The driver was doing something that I was regularly accused of. He was white; the allegation was never said to him.

Private-hire insurance was mandatory for all mini-cab activity but not every driver complied. Law-abiding drivers did not cut corners with their insurance because it was, and still is, the law. If caught by the police carrying paying riders without the appropriate insurance, it's a six-point fixed penalty and two hundred pounds fine. In the case of an accident which injured or killed a passenger in a private-hire vehicle, the driver could be sent to prison. Imagine requesting a private-hire for you and your family which does not have the appropriate insurance but you are not aware of it. Accidents are not regular occurrences but when the nightmare happens, the insurance cover becomes the one and only protection. It's unthinkable to know after an accident in a public transport vehicle that you are not insured; it is nothing but a criminal offence. Before Ken Livingstone became the first Mayor of London, Her Majesty's Government authorised, but not licensed, a taxi trade to operate in the capital. I think it was an ill thought out decision and a very dangerous law to pass. There was a driver whom I always suspected was dodgy. He never stood still and was always looking over people's shoulders. He was given a trip to take a family to their destination. Twenty minutes later, the rider called the cab office and asked to be picked up from the cab she was in. I was asked by the controller to go and complete the trip and he gave me the location of the rider. When I got there, the rider was waiting outside the cab with her children. I asked her if the cab had broken down.

'A police car pulled us over. The driver stopped the cab and ran away. The police chased him and I was left stranded in the cab,' she said.

I was left speechless but didn't want to frighten her with my thoughts about the driver.

'Maybe he panicked. Whatever happened, the cab office governor will let you know,' I told her.

When I returned to the office, the controller knew exactly what had happened because the police officers on the case were already there as part of their investigation. The driver was wanted for murder. In 2000, Ken Livingstone, Mayor of London, started the process of regulating private hire and licensing. We were consequently officially recognised as London Private-Hire Drivers. Although we were primarily given a temporary licence, it was a huge step forward from the previous system. However, if the private-hire trade had been regulated before I joined in 1996, it would have been impossible for me to join. I was a foreign student with a student visa which only allowed me to work for a maximum of twenty hours a week. One of the requirements to become a London private-hire driver was to have no restrictions on the right to stay. I only benefited from the loophole of the unregulated private-hire trade.

In the cab office where I worked, there was overt racism from white drivers towards native African drivers. They also extended their hate towards black riders. The cab office was known for not accepting black drivers for work, and it was only when they were losing many white drivers that the owners started to look outward. Accepting black drivers was to meet the high demand for their riders, and also to accommodate the high demand of black riders. The pick-up areas comprised of a highly populated African community and an established white population. Some of the white riders did not want to be driven by black drivers. It was a dilemma for the owners who wanted to grow their business and could only do so by satisfying their customers, regardless of their ethnicity. Whatever reasons the white riders and drivers had for not wanting to take a trip with native African drivers were something out of the hands of the owner. Riders did not request cabs for fun, they did so to get to their destination and on schedule. Occasionally they are left with no option but to accept any available driver, regardless of their ethnicity. My white riders would formally have a conversation about a bad experience they had had with an African driver. One day, I was given a job to pick up a female rider at her address. On arrival, she was waiting outside her house. I pulled over close to the pavement where she was standing, at a position which allowed her to board my cab from the passenger's door.

'Are you my cab to West Ham?' she asked me.

I confirmed I was her driver. She walked towards the back of my cab, to the rear door of the driver's side, and boarded. She sat directly behind me. Whenever a rider sits directly behind me, it's usually because she wants to travel quietly, and avoid any conversation with me, and I do respect that. We were travelling in a traffic counterflow so I was not driving aggressively as I often did but there was a driver who was driving recklessly. He was in the middle lane when he intended to turn right. When the traffic light changed to green, he deliberately squeezed in front of me and to avoid him, I stopped abruptly. The driver was a cabbie, I knew because he was a native African with two white males in the back of his cab. My rider witnessed the entire incident and was jerked forward in the process.

'Stupid,' she said, referring to the other driver. 'I doubt if he has a driving licence … and he's a cab driver … joke!' she continued.

Until we reached her destination, she didn't utter a word to me nor did she comment on the incident. I concluded that her views towards me were obscured by the experience of someone else. Using one example as a metaphor for a group of people is a very dangerous weapon. An isolated bad experience is transmitted to stereotype everyone in that group and spreads fear. Even riders who have never ridden with me nor had a bad experience with me were sceptical of me while in my cab. It is easy to spread fear into people, and one bad experience will trump the good of the ninety-nine percent. While in Cameroon, I learned about the white culture and attitude from fictional documentaries and films which were a very artificial representation of average whites. Some of my riders also about knew my culture and attitude in the same, based on a film-maker's vision.

Since March 1996 till now, I have transported many riders from my base in South East 17 and the surrounding ends of

London to nearly everywhere in Greater London and beyond. At the time, the two-way control radio was the technology to dispatch jobs within the M25. A Greater London A to Z map to guide me to the rider's destination and back to base was my most-needed work tool. I started driving a mini-cab on the streets of London with Romeo Cars. Our cab office was owned by an African from Nigeria and the riders were predominantly blacks. I learned the topographic map of London during my one year of driving for Romeo Cars. The white riders who required the services of Romeo Cars did not show any signs of discriminatory behaviour. I saw an opportunity to earn a living, and I thought by doing so I was also helping to move people around the then congested city of London. Because basic knowledge or even a topographical knowledge wasn't a requirement to become a mini-cab driver, I asked my riders if they knew where they were going or would seek constant help from the office controller over the radio. The Greater London A to Z map was, to me, like a Christian with his Bible on a Sunday, the most important book in the cab trade then. I learned most of my runs from my paying riders. I took a rider from John Ruskin Street to Gunnersbury Park in Chiswick. It was early evening on a Saturday and the traffic condition was very good. I relied on his directions during the trip.

'How long have you been driving a cab?' he asked me.

'Three months,' I replied.

'Where are you from?' he asked.

'Cameroon,' I replied.

We arrived at his destination.

'How much is the fare?' he asked me.

I didn't know and I didn't want to check my price guide so instead relied on his honesty.

'How much do you usually pay, sir?' I asked him.

He looked at me with a straight face.

'Ten pounds,' he said.

At that particular moment, I believed him because it hadn't taken me too long to get to his destination due to the free-flowing traffic. On my way back to the cab office, the traffic was very slow and I realised the distance was actually quite a distance. I suspected my rider was not quite honest when he told me he usually paid ten pounds for that long trip. With the slow-moving traffic, I checked my price guide and the trip was between eighteen to twenty-two pounds. That native African rider had capitalised on me being a novice on the job and taken full advantage. I wasn't angry at him but told myself not to rely on my rider's honesty in the future. I'd paid my right of passage and from there in, I always double checked the price guide. After the business ran into financial trouble and was forced to stop trading, I joined Briline Cars, which was the nearest cab office. It was like moving into a troubled spot, Little England.

TWO

Back home in Cameroon, I learned how to drive a taxi in the city of Douala city during the political lockdown of 1990 which paralysed the country for nine months. It was a coordinated drive to change the political system. The country was governed by a single political party which allowed the president to be re-elected, unchallenged. The civil disobedience of the entire country was designed to force the leader to organise a national dialogue. However, it was an unrealistic demand of a government who had total control of the power. I, along with many other activists, was very young and had no source of income, investments or savings. The country was in lockdown for five out of seven days with the weekend off for people to obtain essential goods. The traditional yellow taxi colour was replaced with an ordinary colour because the public transport system was completely paralysed.

Before then, in 1987, I learned how to drive through my job as a truck driver's assistant and passed my driving test in 1989. My driving licence came in very handy as it allowed me to drive a personal car which was formerly a taxi. The taxi owner trusted me over drivers who had already got experience in taxi driving because he believed the vehicle was safer with me due to my position as a leader in charge of road blockades. At the time, Douala was a city with a population of two million and taxi drivers had to master a topographical map. I simply operated in areas I knew and I managed to generate an income even during the lockdown period. I pretended to be transporting activists at roadblock checkpoints. Gradually, from that experience, I learned how the taxi trade operated. Although the demands for the national dialogue never materialised, the government gave in and legalised political multi-parties. I continued to drive a taxi alongside my political activity until the next failed electoral attempt in the 1992 presidential election. After that election, my political mentor, a singer by the name of Lapiro de Mbanga, and others of the shadow cabinet, tried to reorganise my political party. The Social Democratic Front chairman and founder disagreed over an internal election to refresh and strengthen the party. It was from then that I stopped trusting career politicians. I did not want to risk my life to replace a leader but rather a political system. We lost the election not because he wasn't popular enough but because his methodology had failed. I wanted democracy, the way it was done in the West where the losing leader actually accepted defeat. They also accepted responsibility for their defeat and consequently stepped aside. I wanted someone with fresh ideas to hold the governing party to account. That part of democracy was absent from a leader who grew in pre-eminence from his democratic rhetoric. His slogan that impressed us, his followers, was "Power to the People" but he failed to act as he was perceived when faced with an internal election within his party. If the political movement I was involved in had succeeded in replacing the then government with Chairman John Fru Ndi at the helm, the current generation would be fighting to replace his government now. The power was never for the people but rather for him. From there on, I decided never to be a political partisan; I will not give my loyalty to any political party and certainly will never become a party member. Politicians speak with forked tongues and have split loyalties. They are the wildest predators in the world, acting as if they are fighting for change but they have never changed anything. We treat democracy as a means to an end in Africa, as if acquiring temporary change will have an impact on our lives. My exposure to western civilisation has taught me that democracy is a process. Even the mother of all democracy has its own challenges with many unsatisfied voters in every election.

Residing in Britain exposed me to the reality of the so-called mother of democracy. When politicians are in opposition, they promise everything to their followers and grow their popularity. As soon as they take office, their popularity starts to drop significantly because their promises were unrealistic. The Liberal Democrat Party was the third one in opposition before holding the balance of power between Conservative and Labour. They promised students that they would protect tuition fees from Conservatives prior to that election. They've always voted against foreign occupation. When they had the opportunity to be in a coalition government, they managed to break all their promises in a single term. When politicians in high office start to disagree with members of their family, it's not because they have developed a new character, but rather they are executing the order of their donors. Political partisans and members are oxygen in the blood of these politicians. They are taken for granted because they defend their politicians' rhetoric and even explain what they meant in their speeches. They are like football fanatics who invest in and support their team unconditionally. Even when their team wins the biggest football prize, they only have alcohol to show their happiness, they can't even touch the trophy. When a politician wins an election, their loyal supporters will gather to listen to their acceptance speech but, apart from those who seek a position in the party, their lives don't change.

I started to plan my exit from Cameroon after staring at a gloomy future. In 1994, after multiple attempts, I finally succeeded in obtaining a student visa thanks to Mama Lucy Njomo. She gave me the much needed help to start a new beginning and I'll be forever grateful for that. She was determined to get me that most-needed break; she challenged my visa's refusal in court and won. She knew I had the potential to excel in life if I was given the opportunity even though I had no formal educational qualifications. She realised that when she travelled with me on a holiday in Cameroon and was exposed to my attitude to life. I was surprised when she told me I could achieve beyond my expectations if I was living in a country with plenty of opportunity like Britain. During her holiday break in Cameroon, many close members of the family were burdening her with their financial situations which was stressful for her. I was to the contrary; I was providing her with a means of transport in my taxi and always bringing her gifts at the end of my shift. Women are more intelligent than the world portrays them to be – they hear the image while we men wait for the sound. When I was leaving the shores of my beloved country and leaving behind my entire childhood memories, I vowed not to engage in any political activity concerning Cameroon. European plutocrats depend so much on the natural resources of Africa; it has become the root of the entire struggle that the continent is going through.

To replace the driver of a slow vehicle when the problem is the faulty machine is a losing battle. African leaders are not the problem. The premeditated historical exploitation of the continent has not changed. Without the coordinated effort of a bigger Pan-African idea, nothing will change and generation after generation will struggle. I would not attempt to drive a vehicle from the outside. I've done my bit and nearly paid with my life. My new chapter is to build a prosperous future for myself and my family. I am proud to have been part of the movement that has given the next generation in Cameroon hope. The multi-party system is a work in progress and a potential to attend their political objectives if they choose to. Fighting to replace a regime I don't want to continue ruling a country I no longer live in is very selfish and irresponsible. To do so would be encouraging others to run the risk while I'm shielding in a safe country with my family. A coordinated attempt to replace a regime is born from disenchanted individual objectives which would lead to a collective objective bubble. Individual drive will become the driving force of the fight, and every fighter knows the risk they are engaged with. I've driven a psychologist who explained to me that speaking on the phone, hands free, is more dangerous than speaking with passengers travelling in the same vehicle. The passenger in your vehicle is running the same risk and can refrain from talking when they can see the driver struggling to avoid danger. The caller at the other end of the phone doesn't run the risk of being involved in the accident and therefore cannot understand the difficulty the driver may be in. Historically, all the freedom fighters I've grown to admire did not liberated their countries from the outskirts. They led the movement from within.

When I was saying goodbye to my friends and family at Douala International airport, I cried. It was my first time leaving the shore of the only country I had ever known and flying into an unknown territory. I had a girlfriend at the time with a relationship which was on and off. We had recently restarted our estranged relationship after a long separation. I knew it was going to be a long time before we would see each other again and anything could happen in between. Most of my friends and family members who had travelled had taken at least five years before their first visit back home. At the airport lounge, while we waited to board, a gentleman walked towards me, and offered me a cigarette. He was smoking, so I took the fag and sat down.

'Is it your first time travelling?' he asked me. 'I've been watching you since the check-in area. Your reaction reminded me of my first ever flight,' he said.

He exhaled a puff of smoke and sat next to me.

'Don't worry about what you're leaving behind … concentrate on the reason for your adventure,' he told me.

I reflected on what the gentleman was saying, I pulled myself together and focused on enjoying my flight. At five p.m., my plane took off from the runway in Douala, Cameroon. I was sitting in the smoking area. I smoked about five cigarettes, one after another, until I fell asleep and woke up when we were landing in Malta. I didn't sleep again until we arrived at Moscow. Along the way, I was reflecting on the things that had caused my life to stall. Why I had to travel over three thousand miles to search for a better life. The first thing I was going to change was my dependency in believing in the fortune teller. I will, from now on, believe in applied science, and look forward to building my life with my own ability. I grew up in the mythology of religion and a witchcraft doctor who did not cater for modernity. I'll always respect my traditional beliefs but in order to progress, I should also respect the culture of my adoptive country. Most of the passengers in the plane were sleeping and the few who were awake were reading. Isolated in my imagined world of thought, I was transiting from a subconscious to a conscious Pan-African. I knew I was going to live in a country in which I'd likely meet Africans from all over the world and I needed to have a different mindset. When my plane landed at Heathrow Airport, I was ready to hit the ground running.

London is one of the best capital cities in the world, not just because of its diversity, but also because of its ancient looks. Driving in London as a taxi driver required skills and an open-minded personality. Just as I did every single day on every trip with every passenger I drove, I want to take you on board this book and share my experiences. I've witnessed the good, the bad and the ugliest experiences in my taxicab. This experience, to me, is bigger than any university I could have ever attended. Although London is the home of every race and nationality in the world, they do not proportionally share the same neighbourhood. Driving through different boroughs, there is always a dominant majority ethnicity which is visibly obvious. The differences are also noticeable by traditional dishes that are served in the ethnic-owned restaurants. The window displays of the clothing shops can also show the density of the ethnic occupants of a borough. The different ethnicities in the thirty-two London boroughs did not happen because the British were kind to foreigners. It reflects the backdrop of the historic colonial influences they had around the world. Conversation in my cab with other ethnic minorities usually started with our individual back story that led us to begin a new life in the United Kingdom. I'm not living in the United Kingdom by accident or because I was just trying to leave Cameroon and adventured somewhere different. My father was a twin and his twin sister had two boys before she passed away. She was very young when she died. By that time, my father had moved to the southwest Cameroon, then under British control. He had no choice but to join the army because it was during the Second World War. Four years later, he travelled back to his village in the western province to see his father and the rest of his family. On his arrival, he was told that his twin sister had passed away, leaving behind two boys. He got married to my mother who happened to be from the same village and took one of the boys back to his new country. At the time there were two parts to Cameroon. The reason my father found himself in southwest Cameroon was because he was running away from the French invasions in his native region. His village was the battlefield for the French invaders. My father was many times mistaken for a rebel by the Gendarmes and also mistaken by the rebels for being an informer. He thought he could find peace in the southwest of Cameroon which was under British occupation after Germany was chased out after losing the First World War. My father's nephew studied mechanical engineering in his new country until he was given a scholarship to study at the London School of Printing. That had created a passage to other members of my family and me to settle here, in the capital city of Britain. Whenever I'm driving in all these different boroughs and seeing all the different races with different cultures, I know there are stories like mine behind everyone.

One Friday afternoon, I was on a trip with a rider from Elephant and Castle to Southall. He was dressed with a traditional Asian costume and I assumed he was Indian. During the sixteen-mile journey, he asked me where I was from. It created the basis for a long conversation. I told him my story up until I started living in London.

'I'm from Africa too,' he said.

I was surprised because he looked Indian and spoke with a British accent.

'I was born in Uganda and came here at the age of one. My parents lived all their life there and returned to the UK when Idi Amin forced them out of the country,' he said.

'Wow! Have you been back there recently?' I asked.

'I have, many times … beautiful country,' he replied.

'My parents never returned. That ghastly decision has never left their minds. They were very comfortable over there,' he said.

He didn't tell me the reason his parents were there in the first place. It wasn't like they decided to migrate from India to Uganda in search of a new opportunity. It was British foreign policy to move people from one of their colonial countries into another. They were acting as sub-colonial powers to build the railway infrastructure to facilitate the exploitation of Uganda's natural resources. In those types of conversation, a lot of information is edited. I knew that because I was born and bred in a country under the control of a colonial French empire and they too used a sub-colonial power. Citizens from a country under their empire were used to facilitate the exploitation of our natural resources. In the case of Cameroon it was the Lebanese who were used to exploit the timber woods that make up the rainforest and that played a vital role in protecting the country from drought. In my rural town of Mutengene, I grew up witnessing countless accidents from trucks carrying timber. The overloaded lorries could not negotiate the stiff descent that led to the town. Mutengene is situated at the foot of Mount Cameroon. For about five miles into my town, there's a continuous descent so that if there are any minor errors from the driver, he may lose control of the truck. The rush to exploit the resources of the rainforest was the only priority for the Lebanese. They cared neither about the drivers of the lorries nor the local people who were caught up constantly in accidents. One of my relatives was a truck driver who used to drive for one of those Lebanese companies. He explained to me how the lorries of those migrants are prioritised over others. They had a direct relationship with the French foreign office who still have military forces in the country. My rider's parents' regret of the Ugandan leader's decision was neither for the love of the infrastructure nor for the good governance of the country. Uganda didn't give equal opportunities to everyone to excel and protect the vulnerable. They regretted the privileged position in their role in the foreign-owned companies as the representative of the colonial exploiters. In the United Kingdom, they were not afforded that privileged opportunity but instead were faced with some resentful racists. I knew he knew the unspoken truth.

I picked up three riders once from separate locations in Chelsea during the campaign of the 2015 general election when Ed Miliband's manifesto included the mansion tax and the debate was on LBC.

'What do you think of that policy?' one rider asked me.

I reflected on what to say because of the area I had picked them up from.

'I totally agree with the policy. Those with broad shoulders should contribute more,' I replied.

'They already contribute more than those on the breadline,' another rider said.

'House prices have increased significantly and it is becoming a problem to first-time buyers,' I said.

'That is not the problem of those who have worked hard to buy their houses,' he replied.

'You mean poor people don't work hard?' I asked.

'The government should help them but not to the detriment of others,' he said.

'The government don't make money from thin air, someone has to pay for it,' I replied.

They had nothing more to say that would convince me.

'Stop debating with him. He probably doesn't own a house,' he told his friend in French.

'Possibly. That makes sense. That policy is for people like him,' his friend replied in French.

I behaved like I didn't understand what they were saying until their destination. Their arguments demonstrated their arrogance of how classism was embedded in them.

There's no other city like London, it is old, historical in every way and is the headquarters of the Commonwealth. Which is the ensemble of countries that Britain has benefited greatly. Together, they've helped industrialise the entire United Kingdom. When I arrived in Britain, from the airport to my temporary family residence at Kennington Oval, I was looking forward to seeing the landscape of the city. For the journey, we took a bus to Victoria and then boarded a black cab to Kennington. When we disembarked from the black cab and walked towards the building, I asked if we had arrived at the London residence. All the way there, I was wondering when we were going to approach the city. I said to myself that maybe it would be after we passed this area. We were crossing the best capital city in the world. I was already in the place I would spend the rest of my life. London is like a very big village. The houses look similar and are all red bricks from the outside. It is the home where the wealth of the world has been one way or the other imported into. When I said London is my residence, I'm talking about my generation, for I personally do not intend to spend the rest of my life here. I was already an adult when I arrived here. However, I've got seven children living here, four were born in London and three in Cameroon. None of them can identify themselves with Cameroon like me. I have no intention of forcing them out of the only country they can fully identify themselves with. They speak English with a London accent and look like Londoners. But of course, extreme nationalist patriots believe that only a white can be

British. I've regularly experienced these situations in my cab office. Their African skin complexion makes them a visible target in the eyes of ignorant self-nominated nationalists who believe in protecting the island. Their generation also were once migrants.

Many white riders have questioned the reason why I had substituted the best and richest continent in the world to make the United Kingdom my home. Some of them were not speaking from a completely naïve position because they had holidayed in several African countries. I drove a rider once who had experienced the blue sky, clean sandy sea, the organic food and the warm and sociable population of African countries. My rider was very positive about his experience in The Gambia.

'I've been to Banjul twice,' he told me. 'Awesome. Every year, when I can afford it, I will make it my holiday destination.'

'Having a holiday break does not paint the full picture of the entire continent,' I told him.

'Which country in Africa are you from?' he asked me. 'It's difficult to tell from your accent.'

'I'm from Cameroon,' I replied.

'I've never been to Cameroon. What is it like?' he asked me.

'Just like neighbouring countries in central Africa,' I replied.

'Have you got beaches there?' he asked.

'It's on the coastline. There's plenty of water, yes of course,' I replied.

'I don't think anywhere else is better than The Gambia,' he said.

I was not insane for moving out from a promised land in search of a better life. I'm just continuing the journey that my father began when the French foreign policy made life unliveable for him. I've also travelled with a rider who actually lived and worked in various African countries. He was very happy and he did not question my reason for leaving the wealthiest continent in search of a better life. He was a petroleum engineer and was employed to work for a multinational company who was exploiting the African oil.

'I've retired now. I spent twenty years in different African countries. Where're you from?' he asked me.

I told him where I was from.

'How long have you been here? I could detect an accent,' he said.

'Over ten years,' I replied.

He nodded.

'Are you happy here?' he asked.

'Yes very much so. Things are far better than my homeland,' I told him.

'Did Africans treat you well?' I asked.

'Better than I anticipated. But home is where my heart is,' he replied.

I dropped my rider on the forecourt of a very nice house. I could only guess that the property belonged to him. My father had ventured for a better life in the southwest region of Cameroon. He was never a coward for fleeing combat. The battle was not a conventional war with a visible enemy. The French used Cameroonians as their foot soldiers to destroy those who opposed the barbaric invasion. Many villagers were burned in their own houses for an ideology they knew nothing about. Whether my grandfather encouraged my father to flee or my father made that decision by himself, I will never know. Until today, the deserted land and the foundation of the houses are still visible.

THREE

A rider who held me to ransom psychologically was a friendly and innocent-looking black woman who was born and bred in London. There was a particular address where drivers were refusing to accept jobs from. However, my motor in life and in this job has always been to mix the rough with the smooth. It's not possible to guess a rider's intention, therefore the job of a taxi driver is a gamble – "you win some, you lose some". The first time I picked this rider up from her address, she looked naïve and spoke respectfully so I had no idea of the roller-coaster ride I was beginning with her. On that day, she booked a cab to go to Oxford Street London West One. The area is famously known as the most popular shopping street in the United Kingdom. On our way to her destination she told me the job was a wait and return. That was music to my ears; because I would get double the fare. Parking is restricted at the west end of Oxford Street but my rider knew exactly where to park, giving me directions like she owned a shop on the complicated roads around there. As I was new to the taxi trade at that time, I was mostly relying on my rider's directions. I waited for about an hour before she returned with four carrier bags full of new clothes. She apologised for the long wait and asked me to take her back home. Upon arrival at her final destination, she paid me the entire fare of thirty-two pounds which included waiting time. When I returned to the cab office my colleague asked me if I had got paid; I was satisfied with the job but surprised that they were asking me about the fare. I didn't understand why. Apparently, in the cab office, the white drivers had a habit of denigrating African riders for being economical with their fares. However, I was better off than those who stayed at base.

Two days later, she called the cab office and requested a ride; she also asked the controller to send her the driver she'd had two days ago. The controller asked me if I wanted to pick her up.

'She requested you in particular,' he said

Having had a good experience with her, I agreed. That day, she took me to three different destinations in London; all shopping locations. By the end of the day, I had spent a total of six hours on this job, making it difficult to calculate the fare. The waiting time far exceeded the job's total journey. I was inclined to calculate the fare on an hourly basis, rounding up the total to seventy-two pounds. My average earning on a weekday at the time was between sixty to eighty pounds. My rider gave me sixty pounds and promised to pay me the rest the next day. She also wanted to book me directly so she asked for my mobile phone contact. Little did I know that I was into a ransom situation. She began directing me to the outskirts of London and to shopping complexes I didn't know existed. I thought she was doing shopping or maybe she was shopping for a famous family. After shopping, I drove her to a very wealthy neighbourhood where there were houses worth millions. After dispatching her goods, she usually called someone in Jamaica, which I knew because their conversation was in the English-Jamaican patois. The call would sometimes last for an hour until she ran out of credit. I thought maybe she had a shop in Jamaica. I was confused about who she really was with all the clothes that she was buying. I drove her regularly for three months and her debt continued to grow bigger and bigger. By the fourth month I began to get really wary because she now owed me over two hundred pounds. Nevertheless, I was encouraged because, overall, I was still better off than if I'd stayed in the cab office.

One day, while waiting for her on a trip at a shopping complex, I was taken aback as she arrived at the cab looking like a pregnant woman. She got into the back seat and asked me to drive away from the area, I kept looking in the rear-view mirror to see what was making her look seven months pregnant in the space of an hour. As I drove out of the residential rural location, she started to remove the most beautiful designer clothes money can buy. I noticed the expensive price tags on the dresses; they ranged between eighty to two hundred pounds. It was fascinating to watch, and surprisingly, she was very relaxed doing it in my presence. That day, we drove to a very beautiful house in our part of town, the famous south London. Before we arrived, she contacted the people to let them know that she had got most of their orders. At the end of that working day, she paid me one hundred and eighty pounds. Although this reduced her debt, it was still substantially high, with around one hundred and forty pounds remaining. Thereafter, I knew what she was up to and I was in a dilemma: keep driving her to her shoplifting adventures and run the risk of becoming a getaway driver or stop driving her and lose all the money she owed me. It was summer and in the cab trade, that period was the least busy time of the year. Most riders are on their summer breaks and with traffic eased up, the rush hours become less busy. After avoiding her for three days, my earnings at the cab office did not amount to the equivalent of one day with her. On the fourth day, she came and waited for me at the cab office. I agreed to go back with her on the condition that she cleared her debts. She agreed and somehow, she cleared her entire debt before we began the day's trip. However, at the end of that same day, I was paid only half of the one hundred and twenty pounds fare. She promised to get it cleared before we began the next day's trip. This was how she kept me hooked for months after months, and I unwittingly became the getaway driver of a shoplifter. I had to insist she booked her job every day at the cab office; I wanted to protect myself against the pre-booking law. The controller was also cool about it because it allowed me to pay the cab office rent without delay. Some days it was the only job that I did from the cab office.

One Friday, it was very warm and we were all over the rural shopping centre. I believe she couldn't find a certain size of a particular dress. She asked me to stop at a shop on Holloway Road, north London. It was an unusually long wait for her but she could not have mistaken my whereabouts because I hadn't moved – I was literally four car lengths away from the shop. Suddenly, a police van stopped and parked right in front of my cab. It was the police van with a transition cell, and three police officers went into the shop. I was anxious and wanted to get out of there as soon as possible because my cab boot was full of her goods. After a while, the police officers walked out of the shop with my rider in handcuffs. As they put her into the van, she looked at me to make sure I was aware of what had happened. I tried to look relaxed but I was shaking and sweating in my cab seat. I drove from Holloway Road to the cab office in complete panic; I didn't know who to explain the situation to. I parked my cab and signed in with the controller to register me as a driver plying for hire. I was trying to cover myself from any police visit with inquiries concerning my shoplifting rider. I did one job and went home – I couldn't drive in the state of mind I was in. When I arrived at the cab office the next day for my normal day's job routine, she was there waiting for me. I thought I was having a dream because she should have been in prison. My cab boot was still full of her stolen goods. She told me she was bailed pending further investigation and she assured me that she would use my service just to sell. She also promised me that she would not go on the road until the police investigation was over.

On that day, my rider booked her trip at the office as directed and off we went. She took me to her clients' houses but all the time she was in between calls to her people in Jamaica and her clients. There was a particular person she wanted to contact and that person was the only one who could provide her with the most-needed tools. The day she finally got hold of that person, she was delighted. Their conversation was strictly business and her contact was and still is a mystery person to me up till I stopped driving her. However frequently I took her to different places, I never had the chance to see this person. From her conversation with this mystery person, I understood that he was providing her with a replacement of her most-needed job equipment. The police seized her work tool while she was being arrested. Only the shop had the equipment to remove the sensor on their goods without damaging the garment. My rider was in possession of the hand-held equivalent of that sensor remover. She was using it to remove the sensor tag on stolen goods and pass through security unnoticed. That hand-held equipment was the key for her shoplifting activities. After trying to get that tool for a week, when she finally got hold of one, the price negotiated over the phone was enormous. The other equipment that helps to dispatch the stolen goods was a film set prop that actors use to play the role of a pregnant character. It gave her a convincing silhouette of a pregnant woman, and it helped her hide the stolen garments. She also used a little game that she played on shoppers who suspected her behaviour. I used to hear her telling her friends over the phone how she would drop a sensor tag inside the carrier bag of the nosy shopper. That trick was to allow the genuine shopper to be stopped by the security guard. Meanwhile, she could secure a clean exit. When it was clear that she knew that I knew what she was doing, she tried to reassure me not to worry.

'I'll always protect you, Andrew ... By doing so, I'll be protecting myself,' she told me. 'I will never run towards your cab if I'm in trouble with those nasty securities. That will not only get you and me in trouble ... they will also seize all the other stolen goods from your cab,' she continued.

From that day, I started planning my exit. I've never been in jail, nor arrested, let alone been through the judiciary. I was not prepared to damage my reputation, just because I wanted to earn a living. Whatever I was owed, it was time to either let go or forever remain her crime enabler and risk becoming a criminal myself.

My rider was the most generous and unselfish African I've known in London. Her generosity was not just to people she knew around her, it extended right up to the people in Jamaica. There was one thing that she did frequently that made me think she owned a fashion boutique into Jamaica. Roughly every two months she was shipping barrels of clothes to Jamaica and travelled during the estimated time of the goods arriving. I later discovered that she was distributing these clothes to disadvantaged children and families over there. During the time I spent with her, I was informed that her parents were not from that island. She did not look like most thieves who dressed in the expensive name-brand garments like she one she stole from the shop. Instead she was always generous to people around her more than looking after herself, and that's why she was always broke. She couldn't afford my fare even though her daily earnings, after selling, was no less than five hundred per day. She was also very protective of African children. One day, I was driving with her and we came across a group of police officers on duty. They were searching a black boy who was in handcuffs. She asked me to stop and offered her support to the suspect, standing as a witness for the boy against the police conduct.

There are many Africans in the United Kingdom who are gifted with physical attributes. My rider's activities proved she had a high intelligence quotient but did not have the opportunity to explore her capabilities. In Africa, the opportunity to study is very limited when a young person doesn't have parents who can pay for their education. The most deprived are orphans who are struggling just to keep themselves alive. In Britain the situation is rather different because the system provides for every child until they're eighteen years old. My rider could not read and write, even though she was born and bred in a country that prides itself on catering for all. Since I started driving cabs in London, I've come across many black youths who cannot read and write. Many of these young people are not in school at the age they should be. It was an opportunity I dreamed of in Cameroon when I dropped out of education at the age of fourteen. Losing my father at a young age meant I did not have anyone to sponsor me. Native Africans are physically strong and intelligent and given the opportunity in any field, they will position themselves in the leading role. More importantly they need to study subjects that are of interest to them and not what their mentors perceive is good for them. Academia is the only true liberation weapon. If many young Africans I came across on the street were given the opportunity to convert their streetwise intelligence into critical thinking, they would achieve highly. My rider was a very intelligent person. She stole from expensive designer clothes shops within highly secure shopping complexes which had cameras and security guards. I saw the ability of a scientist in her if she had been given the chance to pursue her education. Her disadvantaged position in her country of birth connected her with deprived children in Jamaica. She ran the risk of being incarcerated for many years just to get the goods. She then paid for the shipment of the goods, including the payment for the custom duty in Jamaica. All these expenses were generated through her shoplifting profession. Good Samaritans who help others do so under a registered charity organisation. My rider saw herself in those children and families and made it her duty to help with her personal efforts. She may be a shoplifter but her African instincts to other Africans were overwhelming. I would never have experienced the multi-moods of such a colourful character if it were not for my mini-cab adventures. All the knowledge acquired during my taxi driving has contributed in shaping the free-thinking mind I possess today.

A similar rider in activity but different in character was a man who used our service regularly. In his own words, he found me a patient driver and took my phone number so he could request me directly. He was a smart shopper who always dressed as a gentleman; he was always clean-shaven, very respectful and softly spoken. My rider was buying goods in W H Smith and Waterstones then taking them to the corner shops around his neighbourhood to sell them. I became sceptical about this, wondering how someone could buy goods from a supermarket to sell them to a corner shop. After driving him for a while, he started owing me money and slowly the amount built to a massive number. Little by little, his debt reached one hundred pounds just from a daily run which was no more than forty pounds. I also became curious about his business and gradually, my investigation led me to understand his genius mastermind. During a trip, when he left my cab to attend the shop, he left a carrier bag on the back seat. He always sat on the right rear seat to give the impression to patrolling traffic police officers that he was just a rider in my cab and not a friend. (We were both native African.) My curiosity pushed me to look into my rider's belongings where I discovered many credit cards with different names. I thought he was a fraudster at first but with about ten different cards; my suspicion hid a dead end. My rider then returned back to the cab with his goods, supposedly bought by genuine means.

'When you left the cab, you accidentally dropped your bag,' I told him. 'I've rearranged all your cards which were all over the floor.'

He sighed but still seemed relaxed with me although his body language proved he was disappointed with the exposure of the multiple credit cards. Not knowing whether I'd examined the details of his multiple cards, he opened up more about them.

'All those cards are reported lost or stolen,' he said.

At the time, chip and pin on credit and debit cards had not been introduced and users were only required to sign the identical signature as on the back of the card.

'Can you sign every signature on those cards?' I asked him.

'Yes! There's no signature in the world that can't be copied,' he said.

He left my cab to deliver his goods at a local corner shop, a regular destination, and on his return, he asked me to drive to another location where I suspected he bought his drugs from. My rider was a cocaine addict. Having worked in my area for a while, I knew many local drug dealers. I was still anxious to question him about those credit cards.

'If those cards are reported stolen, how do you manage to use them?' I asked. 'Waterstones and W H Smith have not upgraded their computers,' he replied. 'Even when a credit card is reported stolen, their system can't detect it.'

Up to that day, this man owed me ninety pounds but the amount of money I was getting from him was way higher than what I could earn when I worked from the cab office. I continued driving him but his debt reached an unprecedented level of two hundred pounds and I became anxious that I might never get my due back from him, especially as he prioritised his drug dealers. Even though my service facilitated his conning business dealings, his addiction took precedence. I knew this man liked my service because I was very patient with him. What he didn't realise was that my patience was for my service, not with my finance. During one of his trips, he was not in a very good mood. I didn't know why, but he was constantly shouting at his contact. On that day, for the first time, I was exposed to the aggressive side of my rider I never knew he had. I became wary that he might turn that aggression towards me one day if I continued driving him around. It wasn't long afterwards that we started arguing over the debt that was not reducing. One day, after selling his goods at the local shop, he asked me to drive him to his usual destination where I knew he was parting with his money for drugs. I pulled over and asked him to clear his debt. I knew he had sold over three hundred pounds' worth of goods and I had already made my decision not to continue taking him around. I take no prisoners; I wanted to get all of the money he owed me from our multiple trips. He gave me one hundred pounds which only reduced the debt by forty pounds; I took it but insisted on having my debt cleared. After negotiating with me to no avail, he decided to leave my cab and walk away. At first, I wanted to let him go because he was definitely a criminal and I didn't want to get in his way. But then I thought about how I worked for my money and must not let him get away with it, just like he preyed on businesses. I got out of my cab angrily, grabbed him by his trousers and belt and walked him back to my cab.

'Can I have my money, all of it?' I said.

He was speechless because he had never known me in that mood and didn't realise how strong and brutal I could be. A different beast to the gentle cabbie he had known all along.

'What is happening to you, Andrew?' he said in a cracked voice.

'You know I'm going to clear my debt with you. I need you more than you need me and you know that. Come on.'

I knew he had money on him and I was tempted to forcefully grab it and take what I was due. However, I thought it would be too aggressive, especially for a rider I had known for a while. I did, nonetheless, pressure him to clear his debt and he did.

After that scene, I decided not to take him on any more trips. I didn't want to run the risk of driving a crackhead criminal around and, at the end of the trip, struggle to get my money. Many drivers knew he was a problem rider who always had difficulty paying the fare because of his addiction. It angered him when I did not accept his job request; I had already taken my money. I was standing outside the cab office one day, when he walked towards me.

'You think you're tough eh? I'll teach you that nobody messes with me,' he told me.

I laughed at his little threat because physically he could not attack me. I ignored him to avoid confrontation at my place of work. Soon afterwards, I decided to walk up the busy Walworth Road towards a takeaway restaurant. Little did I know that he had three skinhead men covered with tattoos, armed with batons, waiting for me. They chased me onto the busy road to attack me. For the first time in my life, I had to run away from lawless civilians. It put a smile on his face because, according to him, he had got his revenge. The man was from the African continent with a strong West African accent. It is clear that he also migrated here in search of a better life, like me, but although he was potentially intelligent, he was hooked on illegal substances. My job has exposed people's personal stories to me which help me understand what drives them into these risky adventures.

FOUR

MICROWAVE SUCCESS

Many African music artists from Jamaica have used my service. They love to travel with people they can identify with, and African private-hire drivers are highly represented. The use of an ordinary vehicle makes it the right form of transport for them because they don't want attention during their free time. Being African myself made me a perfect match for them. Most Jamaican revolutionary singers are Rastafarian, their song mostly centred on the emancipation and liberation of Africa. Before I started driving Rastafarian singers from Jamaica, I was already re-educated to know what they stand for. People from the island of Jamaica speak English-based creoles which is similar to the pidgin English that I spoke in southwest Cameroon. Driving Beenie Man around London was the most memorable of all. Whenever he was in London, I was his preferred driver. I was also in charge of delivering his food to his place of residence; he trusted me and referred to me as Cameroon. Usually, he travelled with one of his trusted relatives and his bodyguard who always did the talking. Beenie Man appeared very shy but when he spoke, there was so much knowledge in his words. He liked to communicate with lyrical a cappella, and he could go on and on.

Apart from the closeness to one of Jamaica's iconic legends, I witnessed some turbulent moments with the DJ. Once, I took him to one of his shows which was a sell-out at Stratford, East London. However, that night, he had his Rolex wristwatch stolen, Beenie Man did not wear cheap jewellery. I don't know whether he knew the robber or not, but we knew the thief was someone close to him because not everyone was allowed backstage. While the DJ's teams were investigating who might have committed that act, Beenie Man was very upset. I'd never known him that angry while I was his driver. Through his conversation on the phone, I could hear that he was quite clear that he would not wear that watch again, even if it was found. However, in this dark urban world of ours, investigations can be very long and daunting. Rolex watch prices start from £5,000. Beenie Man's Rolex had diamond stones. That alone raised the price to between £15,000 and £25,000, and the gigs that he was doing could not pay for that watch. He did it for his fans but he ended up paying a bigger price. With a situation like that in any other community, the promoters and producers of the singer would have involved the police. Rolex watches are trademarked and each and every one has a serial number registered with the maker to discourage people from possessing a stolen Rolex. Those who robbed the singer were not people who were financially capable of maintaining or servicing the watch. They wanted the bling of the Rolex, not to use it to check the time of the day. Africans living in Africa, America, the Caribbean and in

Europe do not trust the police. The entourage of the singer, including the robbers, will want nothing to do with the police.

As an African, a migrant or child of a migrant, when we call the police as a victim, we are treated as the criminal. I have witnessed this when my then girlfriend, who was from the Caribbean, called the police for her son who was upset after an argument. He was so angry at one point that he punched the bathroom door, creating a hole. At no point was my girlfriend threatened or brutalised by her son. He went into his room and started pushing things around like a big spoiled baby. My girlfriend couldn't control the situation because she was also very angry herself. Out of frustration, she called the police with the intention of calming the situation down. I knew she just wanted him removed from the property temporarily. She was never going to press charges as he was her only child. Before the police arrived, he had already left the house and the situation was very calm. Three police officers barged in as though they had been called for a firearms offence. They were very aggressive, ignoring her when she told them he had already left, and searching every corner of her house. After repeatedly telling the police her son was not in the house, to no avail, she ordered them to leave. She was already upset with her son before she involved the police, but after the intervention she was doubly cross. From that day, I understood why Africans in the United Kingdom were very reluctant to involve the police when they were in trouble within their community and the entire population.

As an African living in Britain, I've encountered my own police prejudgement bias. Every time I was pulled over, it was because of my unsolicited driving skills rather than my personal behaviour. At the time, the use of traffic cameras was not widely use by the authorities. Sometimes, in order to earn more during the rush-hour window, I made unsolicited driving manoeuvres to get out of slow-moving traffic. Mini-cab trade operated from a cab office and pick-up areas were approximately within a two to three mile radius. Wherever a trip took me, I'll have to get back towards my office base to pick up another job. The controller was also putting me under pressure to get back quickly to meet another scheduled booking. Eighty percent of my riders request our service because they are late and they also put me under pressure to get them to their destination on time. I was unwittingly driving under pressure all the time. This affected my driving habits which meant I was flouting the traffic laws most of the time. The police had every right to stop me, issue me with a fine and endorse my licence with penalty points whenever I was caught. On many occasions, that was done with respect and I never thought of them abusing their power because of my ethnicity. I was used to being stopped regularly back in Cameroon when I was driving a taxi in Douala. Over there, police-check stop points were everywhere and I was stopped, on average, five times a day which meant I developed a calm demeanour in front of the police.

However, one time, I was stopped and searched for no reason outside our cab office. It happened after I parked my car and was walking towards the office. The police officer stopped me, questioned me and then searched me. I have never taken drugs and never sold drugs. I was stunned but brave enough to accept being humiliated without throwing a tantrum. The officer's questions were about illegal and fraud-related drugs. It was not intelligence that led to this, it was profiling because he suspected me of two unrelated allegations. The incident happened in front of my fellow drivers and cab office neighbour who knew me. In all the years I have worked in that office, I have never seen the same police officer who happened to be a neighbourhood officer stop a white driver. On another occasion, I was stopped in the Plumstead area when I was going to buy a car to use for my job.

'Someone was robbed here, you fit the description of the robber,' one of the officers told me.

I was flabbergasted.

'You are mistaken, officer. Maybe I'm the one who was a victim of an attempted robbery,' I told him.

I removed a packet of banknotes from my pocket and showed him.

'This is one thousand nine hundred pounds, I'm going to buy a car,' I told them.

They looked embarrassed.

'Have you got the address of the seller?' he asked me.

I showed him the address on a piece of paper which I had written down while on the phone earlier with the seller. The other officer opened the back door of the police car.

'Get in. Let's drop you there,' he told me.

They did it because they were worried that I could be robbed, and to verify whether I was telling the truth. That was not necessary from the police and a waste of time. It was purely police profiling because of my ethnicity. I knew there had not been a robbery in that area and there was no need to stop me. I am African; therefore, I must be up to no good walking in a populated white neighbourhood. On both occasions, if I had shown my frustration, it could have escalated to serious tension between us.

My most memorable police experience which changed my driving behaviour was a lesson from a veteran police officer. He approached me humanely and with the utmost respect I've ever encountered from a serving officer. It was a Sunday morning and I was returning from Stansted Airport. That trip had paid me more than I could earn for the rest of the day. It was quoted at one hundred and five pounds for the multi-carrier trip. With a clear road early that morning, I exited the M11 motorway into the A406 North Circular and then joined the A13 and all along the way my speeds exceeded the national speed limit. Additionally, when I approached the A13, Commercial Road, which is a built-up area with a thirty-mile-an-hour restriction, my speed was nearly double the speed limit. I was driving at forty-five to fifty miles an hour and in doing so, I was weaving in and out of traffic. Behind me was another car doing the same as I was. I assumed it was just another driver taking advantage of the reduced traffic but little did I know it was an unmarked police vehicle. I was eventually pulled over. One of the three police officers stood on the pavement with me and started to question me.

'Do you know why I pulled you over?' he asked me.

'No sir,' I replied. With an innocent face.

'You were driving dangerously and you were being recorded,' he told me.

At that point I was speechless and was just waiting to be fined.

'You're a taxi driver, aren't you?' he asked me.

My private-hire badge was around my neck; I nodded. He pointed at the passing vehicles.

'You see all those cars passing. You probably passed them with your reckless driving behaviour … now they are going to reach their destination way ahead of you,' he told me.

He looked at my private-hire driver's badge.

'Andrew, I can give you a fixed penalty which will cost you one hundred pounds plus three penalty points on your licence … and that will raise your insurance premium for the next five years, but on this occasion, I will let you go on caution. However, you must promise me to adjust your driving behaviour,' he told me.

With a little smile, I said, 'I promise sir.'

On my way back to the cab office, I reflected on everything the officer had said. It had a more profound impact on me than if he had fined me and from that day on, my approach behind the wheel changed. That police officer was a Londoner; I knew that because of his accent. He was an east Londoner judging by his cockney accent and I'm pretty sure his judgement was informed by the people he grew up with. On many occasions when I was fined by other police officers, their accent indicated that they were not from the capital. At the time, I had just had six penalty points after five years endorsed on my driving licence. That did not changed my behaviour behind the steering wheel because I felt the officer could've been a bit more lenient. However, from that day till now I've never been pulled over due to my driving behaviour, and I've not received any fixed penalty points. I've treated my trips from that day as a journey rather than a race. The way I behaved in front of the police is relative to my experience with the cops in my home country. Africans who were born here and never lived anywhere else will not have the same temperament as me. The historical discrimination of being stopped more often than their white peers is what makes their experience with the police challenging.

I'd been driving DJ Beenie Man around when he was in London, and on this day, I was booked to pick him up at the West Sussex Police Station. After landing at Gatwick, the star was arrested by the order of the Child Support Agency. It was for non-payments of child maintenance; an allegation had been made by a mother who claimed he was the father of her child. She alleged the star had not paid maintenance for the child from birth, and claimed he was worth so much money in his hometown in Jamaica. Only two of them would know whether or not the child actually belonged to DJ Beenie Man. How she knew the wealth of a star in Jamaica while living in the United Kingdom was mind-boggling. The DJ had a strange experience in that police van and spoke to me about it in his strong Jamaican accent.

'There's a cell in that police van,' he said.

I laughed, not to minimise his experience but because of the way he said it. He wasn't worried about the problem that landed him in police custody but instead was rather amazed by the police facilities. As well as the pressing problem, there was also the matter of a young woman whom the star was having an affair with who alleged she was pregnant. I don't know how these people's minds work, but he did not look bothered at all. He was just attending his appointment as usual. I took the young woman in question to her hospital appointment. She looked very uncomfortable during the trip, just as every pregnant woman would. This was a woman I had known from when she was a teenager, and I knew what she was capable of. Her ambition was always to become a singer. She gave herself every opportunity by training her voice, and also made contact with people in the music business, but to no avail. She grew up in south London, an area where most of her peers dropped out of school after becoming pregnant. Most of her comrades who became pregnant in their teenage years had only the government handouts and young drug dealers to rely on.

I knew the ambition of this young woman very well; she wanted to be different and always believed she had what it takes to attain her goal. Having the privilege to be close to Beenie Man was a golden opportunity to convince him of her talent after every other avenue had failed. Unfortunately, DJ Beenie has neither a recording studio nor musicians in London who he could link her with. All his studio works were done in Jamaica. I believed that was where their relationship escalated to a different level. Musicians are often known to find themselves in a difficult position with beautiful, seductive women. I also took the young woman's grandmother on a trip. It was a family I knew very well; all five generations of the family were my riders. During her trip, she initiated a conversation about her daughter and the conversation escalated to her granddaughter.

'Have you taken Tricha to the hospital lately?' she asked me.

'I've taken her to the hospital several times. Why do you ask?' I said.

'She told you she's pregnant?' she asked.

'No! She didn't but I knew something wasn't right. She looked uncomfortable,' I told her.

'I went to the hospital with Tricha. While she was in with the doctor, I had a conversation with the receptionist about being excited over her pregnancy. The receptionist was surprised but happy about the news. From that, I knew straight away there was no pregnancy,' she told me.

The British National Health Service has a protocol which can be manipulated. When there's a need to see a doctor, the patient will first see their general practitioner who will examine her condition. If she is concerned whether she is pregnant or not, the practitioner will request an early morning urine sample so they can confirm the pregnancy. The patient can't be asked to come to the surgery very early in the morning to give a urine sample. What the ghost pregnancy manipulator does at this stage is to ask a friend or family member who is pregnant to give her a urine sample. The result will be positive and her general practitioner will trigger a maternity prenatal appointment at the hospital. The prenatal maternity unit will then send the confirmation pregnancy appointment letter. For every problem thereafter, the prenatal maternity unit will be responsible and not the general practitioner. This was how she had been given subsequent hospital appointments and the hospital confirmation letter could be used against the star.

I regularly drove a rider who became close to me. She was a tenant of the local government housing. She didn't have a child which would have put her on a priority housing list.

'Many teenagers who wanted their independence from their parents but were not ready to have the responsibility of bringing up a child were manipulating the system through that loophole. But local government have closed that loophole to stop anticipating independence when teenagers disagree with their parents. In order to qualify for local government housing, a child must be born before the mother can be given priority,' she told me.

While I was on a trip on another occasion with Beenie Man, he was explaining the list of things that the ghost woman was demanding to his relative who was travelling with him. I overheard this conversation, although both being born and bred in Jamaica, understanding them was difficult. The speed at which they spoke meant that I could not keep up fully with their conversations.

'You should see the list of her demands. She wants a sports car,' he told his relative.

He sat on the front seat and his relative sat directly on the seat behind him.

'Hein,' his relative responded.

'She wants a two-bedroom house … a buggy that costs four hundred pounds … so much money for the maintenance of the car … and to decorate and furnish the house,' he told his relative.

'She wants to get rich quick,' his relative replied.

'I didn't bother to read the entire list,' he concluded.

The star did not look like someone who was facing both situations. Just one of those situations would freak me out.

When I took the ghost pregnant woman for her next mystery hospital appointment, she was still acting as a pregnant woman. I just suspended my disbelief and pretended that I was in a theatre. She was acting in my presence because she knew I was Beenie Man's regular driver. Little did she know that her grandmother knew about her ghost pregnancy and the information was circulating already. The star attended the family court several times to face the alleged baby mother representative with her excess demands. She believed that the star was very rich, but Beenie Man's representative argued that the star did not own any wealth in that respect. The claimant was unable to present concrete evidence of the star's worth in his home country of Jamaica. The judge kept adjourning the case until the star was allowed to travel back to his home country. The superstar appeared very wealthy, but he was not financially as free as was perceived. His appearance was deceiving; he spent most of his money on jewellery and costumes for gigs and interview appearances. It's easy to Google the number of music albums the star has sold worldwide and base an argument over his worth on this. In reality, only his accountant can provide his approximate worth through his tax return.

Both women were brought up in Britain's richest city, the capital of the United Kingdom, a city that accommodates more billionaires than any other city in the world. The ghost pregnant woman whom I was familiar with had no father figure participating in her life. The mother was also not really there but was active in her life from time to time as she was brought up by her grandmother. Even the grandmother was a single parent, leaving the ghost pregnant woman to only experience male influence from her associate male friends and boyfriend. As for the mother who alleged her child's father was the star, I never had the opportunity to meet her. However, the resemblances of their adventures were evidence that they shared a similar upbringing. I've always thought of the young ghost pregnant woman as one of the most respectful amongst her peers. The desire to drive a convertible car was part of her dreams. She had a particular sports car in mind long before she met the star. During a trip one day in my cab, a Renault convertible overtook me.

'What do you think about that car?' she asked me.

'Beautiful design. It's an automatic, hardtop convertible,' I replied.

She smiled.

'That's my dream car. I'm in love with it,' she told me.

She lived with grandma, meaning she did not have a house; she dreamed of a car before somewhere to live. She was just learning to drive at the time but already had her eye on a sports car. The situation with the star was a great opportunity to gain her independence from her grandmother and have all her dreams come true at once.

I've known her since she was at primary school and I've always found her to be very intelligent. She always listened more than she spoke, and when she spoke, it was minimal. She used short sentences to make a point; only intelligent people have these skills. I believe if she was patient enough to carry on with her studies as a backup, at the same time keeping her music career dream, she could have become a pioneer of her profession. All she needed was to concentrate her thoughts into a critical educated process. Those two women were in the land of opportunity but could not see a way out of poverty and instead tried to capitalise on someone who was born in deprivation. Their right of birth has given them imaginary dreams that were unrealistic.

Knowing the ghost pregnant woman, she will succeed in her quest for independence but only when she realises her potential. My own experience with my friends and relatives in Cameroon gives me an understanding of the difficulties the star encountered back in his home country. If these two women thought they had difficulties attaining their goal, women in the home country of the star have a mountain to climb.

FIVE

PREJUDICE, FEAR OF THE UNKNOWN

After the private-hire industry became regulated, there was a vast majority of white drivers who did not meet the minimum standards to be granted a private-hire licence. It also affected many mini-cab office operators whose businesses were not financially viable because of the reduction of drivers. Some wealthy businesspeople saw the opportunity and started to buy mini-cab offices, merging them to form a mega office. Investing in any business is always for a better financial return. The new owner who bought our cab office was compelled to rely on mostly native African drivers. The trade became financially viable for drivers and was professionally recognised. My racist white colleague, who often asked me to go back where I came from, was nowhere to be found. Reality has taken precedence, and the white riders who relied on them had reduced choices.

I picked up a rider on a Friday evening. The job was quoted by the controller in the region of twenty-two pounds and was booked as a single trip from Camberwell Green to Orpington. I was on the day shift starting earlier and finishing early evening. As with every Friday evening, it was getting busier, but I was on my last job. When I picked up my rider, he told me that he had to pick up his friend at another address. I was cool with that since it was only a mile away. As a cab driver, I tried to be flexible. After picking up his friend, he asked me to pick up another friend about two miles away. I became wary.

'Don't worry mate, it's on our way,' he told me.

'There will be an additional charge on the initial price,' I replied.

He was very patronising.

'Don't worry, cabbie,' he said.

I picked up the second friend.

'Just the last one down the road … he's waiting outside,' he said.

I looked at the pick-up address, explained the entire journey to the controller over the radio and requested a new quote. The controller was taking a bit longer than usual to get back to me for the complicated trip and the riders started to become irritated.

'Keep driving my friend. We're running late,' he said.

In order not to get the rider who was already irritated escalating to being angry, I started to drive towards the last rider's address. When I picked him up and was ready to take them to their destination, the controller radioed me with a new quote of thirty-eight pounds. The paying rider with his friends could hear the radio.

There was a silence between them.

'That's more than a week's wage back home, isn't it mate?' one rider asked me.

They knew that when the controller gave a quote, there were only two things they could do. Pay the updated fare or create problems by insisting on paying the previously quoted fare. They opted to direct sarcastic comments at my race as I drove them to their destination. What was a quiet trip became an unpleasant journey.

'Which cab office did you use?' the last rider on board asked the paying rider. 'Briline, but it's now owned by Ruskin Cars,' the paying rider replied.

'Ruskin is owned by Roger the Dodger? Greedy black bastard,' said one of the riders.

The second rider looked at me.

'Thirty-eight pounds is too much, mate,' he told me.

He called me mate.

'We're only going to Orpington,' he continued.

'The sixteen pounds charge is for the additional pick-up,' I replied.

I was relieved to have steered the conversation back to sanity. Four big guys who I could attest as people high on drugs and were heading to the public house to get even more drugged up.

'I like Africans who work hard to earn money to feed their family back home,' one of my riders told his friends.

'That's why they work hard … like our driver over here, … isn't it, cabbie,' another one said to me.

It was difficult to listen but I kept my cool. I reminded myself about my goal, do the job and collect the fare at the end of the journey.

'Where are you from, cabbie?' one asked.

'That is not relevant to my ability to do my job,' I told him.

'I'm English and in England we ask questions, not like in Africa where they'll chop off your head if you dare to speak,' he said.

His friends found it funny, and they laughed. The situation was very intimidating. I started driving very fast to shorten the sarcastic remarks' time. They linked the racist conversation to my driving ability when they noticed I was going faster.

'Where did you pass your driving test, mate? I hope you have a British licence and the cab is insured,' one of the riders said.

I did not answer but was conscious that my initial idea of getting them there quickly had backfired. Approaching their destination, I was relieved to know that very soon I'd be dropping off these four guys who, throughout the journey, had made my life a living hell.

Then the rider who initially booked the cab received a phone call and he told me to take them to a different public house. The new destination wasn't far from the first one and under normal circumstances, a change of destination on arrival would incur an additional fare. However, I was just happy to get rid of them from my cab. My job as an assistant truck driver back in Cameroon gave me the option to be part of the loading team. The truck was used to transport 50 KG of cement, rice and cocoa. I was physically and mentally prepared to load and offload my truck to benefit from the additional payment. In addition, to be part of the loading team, I had to be a fighter because the team was made of fighters. At the end of the job, the sharing of the loading money was where the problem began. I stood up many times to people who could eat me for breakfast just to insist on a fair share of my due. People I've confronted in the past were more violent and heartless than the racist riders.

Confronting racism was what I did all the time with my fellow drivers in the office. My cab was where I earned my living and any damage to it would put me out of work temporarily. When I finally arrived at the rider's second destination, they got out, and left the fare on the seat and walked away. While out of my cab, they portrayed themselves as gentlemen. I drove away, knowing that I was a bigger and a better person than them. I'm glad I wasn't educated to hate people without a profound reason. They were using Briline Cars before it was bought by Ruskin Cars. They were used to requesting a white driver for their trips. Not having their choice of driver created a resentment which led to the fare dispute. All four locations I picked up my riders from were in affluent areas with very expensive houses. Whether they were the owners or their parents, I cannot associate them with people from disadvantaged backgrounds. Comparing wages earned here to the one earned in Africa was to degrade my background. If they had been anywhere in the continent of Africa, it was probably for a holiday on Safari to see live animals. There are people who earn more than the average wage in Britain but are living on the bread line. Comparing the living wage is ignorant because it depends on the living standards of the country. I knew they were trying to be sarcastic about how important the fare was to me. They knew the new owner of Ruskin Cars, although he was an Afro Caribbean, was born and bred in the United Kingdom. He was a successful businessman and the hateful racism towards him was born from a jealous mindset. Roger's mother and father were still married and lived together for all the time I'd known them. He was a handsome, black man and greediness can be associated with every successful businessperson on this planet. I was no fan of Roger's business philosophy and will never use his model, even if it would help me achieve more than my potential. He was using the ideology of very selfish capitalists and believed money was made just for him and was never satisfied. Although he was brought up in a dangerous estate, he went from nothing to become an affluent wealthy businessman. He built his wealth through fruit machine games in public houses. Those public houses were mostly owned by whites, and in order to convince the white landlords, Roger used his white friend as the negotiator who was likely to be accepted. He became a private-hire operator when public house landlords decided to use their own fruit machine games. The smart thinker that Roger was is the reason why he became the youngest, most successful black businessman in the area. He gave wisely, just as most businesspeople do. In other words, he invested in people and expected a profitable return. My riders did not like him because he was not a drug and drink friend; he had nothing in common with them. Roger was the first African I've known in Britain who owned the best luxury cars, was a model in designer gear and wore the most expensive watches.

Years later, Roger declared bankruptcy and his affluent business as a private-hire operator was put into administration. Most of us the Africans drivers who worked for his company were not surprised. Roger's quest for his capitalist business model reduced his company to ashes. He invested in a political party in order to be in front of the queue for local government contracts. That meant the traditional private-hire sector of the company was ignored. The riders who relied on their local cab office for their trips were neglected and were left with no choice but to rely on other cab offices. He prioritised the government contractual agreements because there were more financial returns in that department of his business. The transportation of school people living with disabilities to school and back on council contracts took precedence over mini-cabbing. Although the business grew faster than any other rival operating with similar trade, he became artificially powerful and isolated himself even more from his people. He went from being a friendly boss to someone unrecognisable. Just to have a meeting with him regarding a workplace issue became very difficult. Classism was visible between us. He was above the law and did not settle his parking fine with the local government because he was dealing with the political leader of the Borough. Unfortunately, the particular political party he invested in lost an election and the newly elected political leader saw him as a rival. None of his contracts were renewed and he was forced to face the depth of his parking fines. The penalties and administration cost, including bailiff fees, increased his debt significantly which forced his business into administration.

He changed the name of his private-hire business and tried to restart the company. By then, most drivers had left but I was part of the few loyalists to his reinvented ideology. Most riders had already found a mini-cab office which respected their loyalties. One can never run away from your shadow, Roger learned that lesson the hard way and unfortunately there was no room to turn the clock back. He wanted to go fast; he went alone and ended up in no-man's land. If he'd confined his business dealing with people around him that had his best interests at heart, he would have still been a pre-eminent businessman today. Bourgeoisies use democracy as their tool to protect their wealth. Novice businesspeople like Roger ignored the risks of politics and business. Career politicians know the unpredictable nature of their profession because they know it's impossible to live up to their rhetorical promises. Their split personalities make it difficult to execute their electoral promises and the ones of their big donors. Many career politicians are known to secure greater contracts after their political ambitions hit the rocks. Nick Clegg was the leader of Liberal Democrats, and the deputy prime minister of the coalition government. After five years in government, he lost the majority of their seats, including his own. His political career came to a premature end at a young age but he is now in his dream job at the head office of Facebook in America. Businesspeople like Roger don't have that luxury and should rely solely on growing their business through their personal efforts.

My time driving at Ruskin Cars was my most memorable because of the mixed calibre of the riders. Prejudice is not endemic to one race; I encountered unacceptable behaviour in my job. Some riders assumed everyone from the same ethnicity held the same view. I was driving along Standford Hill with two African riders one Friday morning. There were a lot of Jewish people walking around dressed in their religious attire. One of my riders started making fun of them and his friend or relative thought it was funny. He felt he needed to impress him even more or wanted to prove how courageous he was. He wound the window down to have them clearly in his sights.

'Oi,' he shouted. 'Why do you dress so primitive? That's so eccentric,' my rider shouted at the passer-by.

They briefly looked at him and continued their journey.

'This is London, not Israel,' he continued his unprovoked attack.

'Please stop insulting these people. Whatever issue you have with them, a random provocation is not called for,' I told him.

'Are you Jewish? Maybe you're a black Jew,' he asked me in a mocking way. 'If you want to behave that way to a passer-by, it shouldn't be in my cab. My registration is my identity,' I told him.

'Just shut up and concentrate on your driving,' he told me.

I kept my cool until their destination and prayed for them to leave my cab without physically attacking me. They were just troublemakers who wanted to attack people without justification and the majority of Jewish people in the area became their victims. The behaviour they portrayed on that trip did not start in my cab but rather before they requested their ride.

There were some awesome riders who gave me the pleasure of forgetting about the awful ones. The longest distance I did during my time driving a cab was a trip from King's College Hospital to the University Hospital of North Durham via Portsmouth Regional Hospital. I was taking a team of NHS medical staff back to their base. The air ambulance that dropped them couldn't wait for the surgeon and his team to transfer the patient. During the long drive back, I had a conversation with the three female medical staff. Their surgical gowns were different in colour. The two white women had the same colour surgical gowns and the African woman who was from Zimbabwe had a different colour. I kept referring to the two white women as doctors and to the African woman as nurse. After repeating the same mistake on three different occasions, the African woman told me she was a surgeon. In a polite manner, she said her two colleagues were her theatre nurses. She was using medical terms during her contribution to the conversation that the other two were not using. I don't know why I thought the hospital would deploy two surgeons and one nurse to transfer a patient. Stereotyping is a subconscious disorder that can be associated with dementia; it creeps in unnoticed. I'm very much aware of the old view of thinking that male medical personnel are likely to be doctors and the female are likely to be nurses. I was very ashamed of myself after she corrected my remark, but it was a series of prejudgements I've been trapped into.

Driving young people living with disabilities helped me understand how life can be challenging for some families. Without the Ruskin Cars' contract with the local government, I wouldn't have known the obstacles these families faced. The majority of the people were transported by specially adapted vans, with wheelchairs accessible for those with physical disabilities. Those with invisible disabilities were using ordinary taxicab like mine for their round trip to school. My previous experience with these people had always been under the supervision of their parents. On school runs organised by the local authorities, they are provided with an escort. The escorts themselves were not accustomed to the people's needs and unpredictable behaviour. My job, according to the office, was just to drive because the young school people were under the care of the escort. But it was never as straightforward as it sounded. Throughout my time transporting these people, I was regularly given a new set of runs. At first, I didn't want to commit to any particular run because it wasn't something I initially went into taxiing for. My first troubled school run on that long running contract with Ruskin Cars was a young African boy. I was not made aware of his condition and, unusually, I was given two escorts for the run. When I arrived at the school, he was brought out of the building by two special needs teachers. The two escorts held the boy by his upper arms, and one escort got into the cab before letting the boy in. The second escort sat next to him, putting him in the middle. During the trip, he was jerking his head forward and backwards all the way until we reached his destination. While taking him out of the cab, there was a lapse of attention which briefly freed the boy from both escorts. He jumped out of the cab and ran down to the bottom of the road. The two escorts ran after him with great anticipation of catching him before he accidentally hurt himself. The mother was waiting outside her house for the handover of her child and witnessed the scene. Eventually, they were able to catch up with him and took him safely home without any major incident. The mother had not looked relaxed when her son was being handed over by the escorts.

That was my very first school run and my first scary moment. The boy had ADHD (attention deficit hyperactivity disorder) which the escorts knew.

'What happened to that boy?' I asked.

'He's just energetic for his age,' one escort responded.

'He looked like he was on a running track,' I said.

'He knows the area very well. That's where he lives,' the other escort responded.

'You look exhausted. That's your daily exercise,' I told them with tongue in cheek.

'It's not the first time he has done that … this is the third time that it has happened with me,' he replied.

'The mother of the boy was watching her son being chased,' I told them.

'Yes. She wasn't happy but she knows how difficult her son is,' one escort replied.

After that trip, I asked the controller to give me another run. I told him that particular run should be done by the company vehicle. I took that decision to prevent damage to my cab in case the physical behaviour occurred in my cab. There was a school run to a boarding school for people living with deafness in Brighton and Hove. I was assigned to take the people to school on Monday morning and bring them back to their residence on Friday evening. The office didn't tell me the health condition of my passenger and again, I was left to discover it during the trip. I picked up the escort and she directed me to the address. As they boarded my cab, they greeted me politely and I returned the compliment. It was a long journey so I introduced myself.

'Hi, my name's Andrew. I'm your new driver,' I told them.

The girl directly behind me looked at me with a smiling face.

'Hello, I'm Fiona,' she said.

The second girl also had a smile on her face.

'Hello, I'm Nickita,' she said.

At this point I realised I wasn't dealing with people like the previous character. There were always traffic jams towards the M23 and my escort had her newspaper to look at in between talking to the girls. I asked them how long they'd been attending their school. I liked the run and wanted to develop a good working relationship with them. On our way back to London, just with the escort, we talked.

'What's the disabilities of those girls?' I asked the escort.

'Deafness ... they can't hear sound,' she replied.

'How is that true? We were interacting verbally,' I said.

'The school we just dropped them at is a special needs school for people living with deafness,' she replied.

After knowing them for a little while, we had another conversation on a Friday afternoon during our trip back to London.

'Do you recognised my voice?' I asked Fiona.

'No!' she replied .

'How come you're responding to everything I'm saying?' I asked.

'By reading your lips' movements. That's our main lesson,' she replied.

It was a very easy school run with the school people presenting the behaviour of little angels. My problem was that it was only two days of the week, leaving me with three days without a school run. The escort was a very nice white middle-aged woman who had been doing the run for over fifteen years.

One Friday afternoon, just the two of us were travelling from London to pick up from the school. At the time, Zimbabwe was making the headlines on every media around the world. The two opposing political parties were fighting to gain power and the land reform was used to divide the country. The British tabloid printing press relegated their internal dogma to their back pages and suddenly became interested in the sovereign African state. The escort was listening and reading the British version of the political arguments which was from a biased viewpoint. The British historical link to the colonialism of the country was the cause of the problem. She knew that I was from Africa but she had no geographical knowledge of the different areas of the continent.

'Where will the people in Africa live if they seize the land? And the white Zimbabweans decide to destroy their buildings?' she asked me.

She actually believed that the cities' infrastructures were owned by white Zimbabweans.

'The land is of no use if the residents don't have the means to exploit it,' she continued.

I didn't know what to say to her because the media had reduced her to thinking that Zimbabwe was another name for Africa. Our journey was long, and I used the otherwise boring trip time to explain to her that Zimbabwe was one of fifty-four countries in Africa.

'There are black Zimbabweans who are far richer than the minority whites,' I told her.

From my experience working with her, I don't believe that the escort had any racist thoughts. Her views were obscured by the newspapers she was reading during our long trip to the school. Most of the school people she was responsible for were blacks and she treated them with respect at all times.

My close colleague had a school run which he did for about four months. He went on holiday and didn't return in time for the beginning of the school term. The transport department in charge of the run called me and proposed that I did it on a temporary basis until he returned. After my Brighton and Hove run, I covered the new vacant school run. The trip was to a rehabilitation centre for people who had been excluded from mainstream school because of their behaviour. They were three boys: one white, the second was mixed heritage (both were cousins) and the third boy was black. The escort who looked after them was a Muslim woman from Somalia. The first time I picked them up, the black boy did not want to sit with his peers on the back seat. He asked the escort to swap her seat with him which she did. I was not comfortable with this because I wanted to avoid any unnecessary allegation with him being so close to me. The next day, I told the black boy to sit in the back seat with his peers. He did but was not comfortable and throughout the trip I could see some physical movements from the three of them. Unfriendly finger gestures were exchanged between them without actually poking or hurting each other. One afternoon after school, the escort and I were running late to pick them up. When we arrived, they were waiting at the entrance of the school and from a distance we could see that they were in a confrontation of words. The black boy was not happy for some reason. The white boy, who usually sat in the middle seat, separating the mixed race boy from the black boy, sat at one side. The black boy was looking towards the window and his body language was clearly highlighting his discomfort. During the trip, the mixed race boy was poking the black boy continuously. I witnessed the scene properly and knew it was an unprovoked attack because the black boy was not retaliating so I found a safe place on the single carriageway and parked my cab.

'Bullying has no place in my cab and it must stop from now on,' I told the mixed race boy.

The boy looked shocked. From then on for a week or so, the black boy was comfortable during the journey to school. Three weeks later, the cab office received a report complimenting my run by the local government representative. But I was called to the office to answer a complaint made against me from the mother of the mixed race boy. She alleged that I was bullying her son. I wasn't worried because the escort was there to explain exactly what had happened. The bullying was the reason my colleague did not return to the run when he came back from his holiday. The escort was relieved with my approach on dealing with the boys which made her working experience enjoyable again. I didn't see the mixed race boy as a problem because he behaved perfectly thereafter until the mother intervened on behalf of her child.

SIX

WHERE THERE'S MONEY, EVERYONE'S A STRANGER

The hardest part of my job has always been to get my fare at the end of the trip. There was a rider whom even the cab office controller suspected didn't have the means to pay for the ride but for some unknown reason, he didn't ask the rider to pay upfront. The controller radioed the next driver on the list. I drove my cab in front of the cab office and he radioed me again and told me to collect the fare before beginning the journey. At that moment, the rider was close to my cab but he didn't hear the controller's message. Before he got in my cab, he had already engaged me in a conversation.

'You alright cabbie? I'm running late. I'll give you a good tip if you get me there on time,' he told me.

The handbrake was still up and the gearshift was in the P position. He looked at me as if I didn't understand English.

'The fare is fourteen pounds,' I told him.

'Yes, that's not a problem, I do this journey all the time,' he replied.

'The controller asked me to collect the fare upfront,' I told him.

'You're joking. He didn't say that to me when I was in the office,' he replied. 'It's the rule. I'm just doing what he asked me to,' I told him.

'Listen big man. I'll give you the money when we arrive. My girlfriend is waiting with the money,' he told me.

I shook my head.

'Go back in the office and ask the controller. If he accepts, I'll take you,' I told him.

He got out of my cab and, still with the door wide open, he looked at me.

'You lot are fucking jokers. You've wasted my time for nothing. Fucking illegal immigrant,' he ranted at me.

How was driving a pre-booked taxicab connected with illegality? My rider was a black man from the Caribbean. Although he was also a migrant, according to him, I was an illegal resident in our adopted country. Our cab office was based near East Street Market, the birthplace of Charlie Chaplin. There were many businesses around the area attracting many shoppers and also those who usually shopped without the means of paying. At that time, the private-hire sector was authorised but not licensed. If a rider does not have the means to pay for their ride at their destination, the police could not force them to pay. After losing cab fares from riders who just walked away at their destination, I became wiser.

Tuesdays were generally quiet for the taxi trade. I had waited for over two hours for a trip, when a woman walked into the cab office and requested a ride. The trip was a long journey with a wait and return which was classified as a very good job. I was the next driver to go. I was in the cab office at the time of the booking so we walked together towards my cab. She looked at me with a smile.

'Can we drive through Missenden, please? I want to pick up my sister. We're going together,' she said.

I nodded. Missenden was a massive block of flats, but when her sister came out, I knew her. She was a regular rider who used our cab service and my worries about whether my rider was a fare dodger were appeased. The trip was initially to Hendon and back which was quite a long way. I usually asked base riders to pay upfront, but for some unexplained reason I didn't. During the trip, from my rider's conversation, I realised that she was going to collect some gold jewellery from her business partner. Her partner had just arrived from Indonesia where they buy merchandise to sell in the UK. When we arrived at the destination, my rider's business partner boarded the cab. I was then asked to drive them to Beckenham which was way past our cab office. My rider was worried about the scheduled time of arrival at the next destination and from their conversation which was in their dialect, I did sense tensions between the three. Through the little broken English that was spoken between in dialects, I could understand that they were disputing the content and quality of the gold jewellery. I was already three hours into the job and thinking that I could not be paid was unthinkable. But I reassured myself about the presence of my rider's friend whom I knew was honest. We arrived at her second destination at Beckenham, where they all got out and went into a private residence. I waited anxiously in my cab. After about thirty minutes, my rider and her friend came back and asked me to drive back to Peckham.

My anxiety became worse as I was driving towards the third destination. I was constantly checking my internal driving mirror to evaluate the facial expressions of my rider. The two women did not look convinced about the quality of the jewellery. I arrived at the third destination; it was a cash converter shop and I guessed they were going to exchange their goods for cash. At this point, I was already five hours on that single job. I found myself in a situation that could make or break my day whichever way the rider settled my fare. After waiting for forty minutes, they left the cash converter's shop with facial expressions that made me believe something was not right, and boarded my cab.

'Let's go back to Beckenham,' my rider instructed me.

I didn't want to give her the benefit of doubt anymore.

'Can I have some money, please? I need to put petrol in my cab,' I told her.

'I do not have cash with me, but at Beckenham, I'll give you money for petrol,' she said.

She didn't even ask me how much I was due, and I took that as a sign that I might not get paid for the job.

'Your fare is one hundred pounds. I want the money now before I continue,' I told her.

She took out a gold necklace and gave it to me as a guarantee that I would get my fare at her final destination. My suspicion grew even more. Her sister looked disappointed. 'Please, sir, drive to Beckenham. That's the only way she will be able to pay you,' she told me.

I was already trapped because I should have asked for my fare upfront. I drove to Beckenham hoping to get my complete fare. I waited for another thirty minutes for them to come out. While I was waiting, I checked the necklace she had given me as security and it was fake. My rider and her friend returned and asked me to take them back to her house at Elephant and Castle. I asked again for my fare and she had no reply. I knew my suspicion was spot on. I'd lost a day's work and there was nothing I could do. I radioed the controller and explained the situation. He was mad at my rider over the radio but it was just hot air. My rider was an ambitious con artist who wanted to get rich and I was used as a facilitator for her unsuccessful venture. I told her to get out of my cab after it was clear I wasn't going to get any money. Her friend stayed in the cab, begging me to take her back to the cab office area. With just the two of us on the way back, she told me that her friend had recently spent nine months in a mental health hospital. It was a sad day for me but I learned a lesson by losing not just a day's work but burning the fuel in my cab in vain. These are the type of jobs that give cab drivers high blood pressure but I was more resilient to the ordeal.

Arguments between riders and I usually start with the pre-arranged or quoted fare. Most riders request their trip from the comfort of their house. Due to unpleasant experiences, some riders want to know the fare before their ride. The problem is that areas within a single post code can vary between one and three miles. Private-hire cabs are not allowed to use a meter, but must use a price guide from the cab office location. The single postcode of South East 15 is referred to as Peckham, and many riders have taken advantage of the large territory. When the rider's destination exceeded the fare quoted by the cab controller, some riders will just pay the additional fare. There are also those who want to stick to the estimated fare, regardless. I was given a trip from Portland Street SE17 to Peckham; the trip had a quote of four pounds. However, from where I picked up my rider at SE17 to the final destination in Peckham, it meant the fare quoted was exceeded. From my estimation, the cost to her final destination was seven pounds. My rider gave me four pounds. I didn't accept it.

'This end of Peckham is seven pounds. This is Nunhead,' I told my rider.

'The controller told me four pounds ... you can ask him if you want,' she replied.

She was not happy to pay the increased fare, and I sensed trouble. I radioed the controller and requested the exact fare of her final destination. Over the radio, she could hear the controller quoting that end of Peckham to be in the region of seven pounds. Because the adjustment of the fare was done by the controller, it cut out the argument. She phoned the controller herself and told him that I had used a longer route to her destination. I didn't hear the response of the controller, but my choice of route made no difference to the fare. Private-hire fares are set from the Automobile Association's shortest route. My rider was angry not just at me for initiating the dispute but also at the controller for not being accurate with his quote.

'You Africans love money like mad,' she insulted me.

'No problem, just give me the fare. I have to go,' I told her.

She searched her handbag and it seemed there was no more money to complete the fare.

'For crying out loud ... These refugees worship British pounds,' she said

'Who are you calling refugee?' I asked her.

'Aren't you a refugee?' she asked me.

My rider was a black woman born in the UK.

'What are you? Is this your country?' I asked her.

'Yes, I was born here. I'm British,' she replied.

'What's the use of your Britishness if you can't even afford a cab fare?' I asked her.

My rider's relative was waiting outside the destination with the door open. He was wondering why she was taking so long with me. He walked towards us with an angry facial expression.

'What's going on?' he asked.

'He wants to overcharge me,' she told her friend.

'How much more does he want?' asked her friend.

'Three pounds. I thought I had some coins in my bag, but I can't find any,' she replied.

Her friend gave her three pounds and she threw it on the front seat.

'I'll never use your cab office again,' she told me.

'Who needs useless riders like you. The controller knows you're a troublemaker. I don't think he'll ever send you a cab,' I replied.

Her friend was eager for them to leave the scene, but she had a surprise for me. She walked towards the passenger's door.

'Go back to your backwards country, you fucking refugee,' she shouted at me.

I made a face at her as a response gesture. She then spat at me. I was very alarmed at her strange behaviour. I quickly bent towards the steering wheel and escaped the majority of her saliva. I saw a native African who thought she could erase her African roots out of existence. She seemed completely ignorant to the fact that she was living in a country with a constituency that regularly asked people like her to go back where they came from. Racists don't really care about their victims' place of birth. As an experienced driver, I knew my rider was a case when, during the trip, she was arguing with the route I took, even when I explained the reason for that choice. She was also stressing about what other drivers were doing. Luckily, those situations were not the frequent behaviours of ninety-nine percent of my riders.

After that job, the controller was trying to make up for the loss of working time with my previous rider. Two hours later, he gave me a trip which, in hindsight, looked like a good job. It was a bright Saturday afternoon. I drove a people carrier (MPV) that was licensed to carry six passengers. When I arrived at the pick-up point, the riders were three adults with seven children aged between four and seven. People carrier jobs are often quoted at a fare and a half but although I was being paid more than a regular trip, my licence only authorised me to carry six riders.

'My private-hire insurance forbids me to exceed the allowed number of riders,' I told the three adults. 'You will have to call for one more regular cab for the additional four riders.'

'We're only three adults,' she said. 'The children do not occupy much space, they can all fit in the cab.'

'In a personal car, you can take that risk and get away with as many people as you see fit, but insurance for commercial use is different. The space to fit everyone in the cab is not the problem, but the insurance should cover each rider in the cab,' I continued.

'Don't worry, my brother. We'll not have an accident, God is in control,' she told me.

It sounded to me like she had disregarded everything I'd told her. Just because she didn't want to pay more for her trip, God will give me an invincible ten passengers private-hire and rewards insurance.

'I don't do God at work. The law of the land takes precedence over what God may or may not do,' I replied.

Twenty minutes later, she booked another ride and I carried the six riders allowed. I eventually took four children in my cab, plus one of the mothers who sat next to me and another mother in the middle seat. I knew they were not happy riders but I kept a serious expression and I knew there was not going to be any conversation between us. Some riders are happy with my service and some are not, that's part and parcel of my job. The mother in the rear seat spoke to her sister in French.

'Whenever I request a cab and I get a black driver, there seems to be trouble, always. If it was a white driver, he would've allowed all of us in his cab,' she told her friend.

I knew that statement is not true, any cab driver who accepts more riders than their insurance allows is definitely not insured. She sucked her teeth, folded her hands and stared at me. She said in French to her sister.

'Black people with their black hearts,' she continued. I know what she meant. That insult is widely used within the African community.

Her accent indicated to me that she was from the Ivory Coast, a country from which I happened to know many citizens. It was the first time I had been on the receiving end of such a strange remark from someone in that country. I've received worse insults than that, but the reason I was driving them was to get paid at the end of the trip and that was the only thing that mattered. The mother in the front seat was responding with body movements. I thought that maybe she knew that I was right.

She continued in French to her sister. 'He is very ugly.'

I looked at her through the driving mirror, our eyes met, and she quickly looked away.

'Tell your sister to stop insulting me,' I told the mother.

'How do you know she is insulting you?' she asked me.

'Her body language … I can tell from her body language,' I told her.

'Keep driving. We're just having a conversation … or is it forbidden to chat in your cab?' she asked me.

Her sister sucked her teeth.

'Ugly, dirty, black … what's his concern about our conversation,' her sister responded in French.

I stopped my cab and asked her to refrain from the continuous abuse on me.

'What's wrong with you? I told you that she is not insulting you,' she replied.

I responded in French.

'There's no need to continuously insulting me while I'm giving you a service,' I said.

Our respective countries share a lot of internal tribal divide and similar political struggles. I have grown up with people with similar behaviour from my childhood. Private-hire operates on a restricted zone. We were conditioned to rely on the same riders. I had no choice but to exercise a bit of patience with them because we might meet again. In different circumstances, we could have a pleasant experience. Her sister in law who was acting as her barrister felt so ashamed and tried to apologise. She was from Nigeria but had lived in France for a while so she understood I was being insulted.

'I didn't make you take two cabs because I wanted you to spend more for the ride. It's the law,' I told them.

I continued to their destination, and she didn't utter a word until she left my cab. I wasn't angry at her because I do not know what has happened to her before we met.

Two weeks later, I saw the rider who had insulted me near the cab office. A bond was formed between us; we spoke in French and we became friends. After that, she requested my service through the cab office each time she needed a cab whenever I was around. We Africans are so proud of our colonial divides and enjoy speaking the European language, and sometimes we forget that it is a foreign language. I did not know whether all the children in my cab understood French. They were all black children who were witnessing a black man being denigrated. Their parents associated the dark skin complexion with ugliness. During the trip, the children were very quiet. I don't know if those children were affected by this conversation. However, they would remember the scenario for a very long time and process it to be their reality. My riders were not thinking of how their actions could affect the children at the time. They were completely unaware that the children were listening to the arguments.

Later on, when we became friends, she told me that the little albino girl among the children was her daughter. She was a very pretty, respectful and friendly little girl. She told me that her family had a trace of albinos, a minority group who are overtly discriminated against in Africa. Although my family does not have a trace of albinos, I was brought up with two separate albinos' families. I attended my primary school from my early years with an albino family friend; our parents were very close. The other albino family member was the namesake of my niece. Whenever I was not at home, the first place to look for my whereabouts was at her house. At my young age, I was conscious about the view of other members of our community who had little or nothing sociable to do with the albinos' families. I and my family were not colour blind to our different skin complexions but had no reason to discriminate against one of the best behaved families in the community. My rider has undoubtedly witnessed close family members discriminating against her daughter. She should be well aware of the pain that it causes when someone is being discriminated against or judged negatively because of their complexion. As human beings, we all have our moments in life which we wish that could be erased from history. That moment could also be the actuality that shapes our future behaviour and improves our life and others around us. That day was a test of my mental capabilities to know if I will come out sane whenever I decide to give up cabbing. Retired cab drivers often refer to their profession as brain damage because of these types of scenarios that they have to deal with.

SEVEN

Twenty-five years ago, every mini-cab office dispatched their jobs through a controller on the radio, by phone or verbally, if the driver was in the office. At the time, every cab office had a rest room for drivers, mainly to use during quiet hours to refresh themselves or even to have a nap. Any system that requires a human being to have full control to enable its functionally must realise that there's room for genuine error and bias. In our cab trade, the job dispatcher, who was known as the controller, favoured some drivers over others. Our controller had friends among the drivers, those who bought him lunches, cigarettes and drinks were prioritised on trips which were deemed to be good. During busy times I noticed that cab office controlling was one of the most difficult jobs in the trade. Our controller was the bridge between the drivers and riders. When he dispatched a job and the rider could not connect with the driver, the riders would put him under pressure.

On this occasion, I was given a job at an address which was a building among others in an estate. I drove into the estate and parked in front of the building. My rider was waiting at the front while I was complaining to the controller that I could not see him. The controller was relying on the information I was providing of my whereabouts. The rider was running late and that caused him to be angry and abusive towards the controller. The building had two entrances and where I was parked, the flat number sign was missing. The rider was at the next entrance of the building but unaware that I was at the wrong entrance. It was the quick thinking of the controller who suspected that I was at the wrong entrance and directed me to the right place. The rider was on the phone with the controller when he boarded my cab, still very upset about the delay.

'I'm going to miss my train because of your ineptitude. If I don't make it in time to the station, I'm not going to pay for this cab,' he told the controller.

He was going to King's Cross Station. I wasn't sure if I could make it to his destination on time and didn't want to drive him for free.

'I'll try and get you there on time, sir, but please can you pay me the cab fare so that when I arrive, we will not have to argue,' I told him.

'Just drive before I lose my temper. You make me late and then I have to pay upfront because you don't trust me or what?' he replied.

The rider was too upset for me to reason with, so I stayed put and allowed him the time to make a decision one way or another. He realised I wasn't in a rush to drive to his destination as he had ordered me, so he removed the money from his pocket and put it on the front seat.

'Can you drive now, please!' he ordered me.

I started my cab and luckily, I didn't hit any traffic jams on the way and managed to get him to his destination on time. A journey that usually took forty-five minutes, I did in thirty. When I started my aggressive driving, my rider wore his seatbelt because I was breaking all the driving regulations. When I returned to the cab office, the controller, who had received much abuse from the rider, wasn't happy with me.

'Did you get him there on time?' he asked. 'I got a lot of abuse from the customer because of you. You've been working here long enough to know the different flat entrances of that building,' he continued.

I had nothing to reply to his rants. I had learned from my mistake and didn't want to extend the palaver of that trip.

'Give me a break, please. We all make mistakes sometimes,' I told him.

'That rider requested Chris. He wasn't around and I put my trust in you because I thought you were the only one with a brain amongst you lot … but you let me down,' he told me.

My rider was a white male and Christopher, who he had requested, was also a white driver. I knew the controller would never give me a trip from that rider again. He would rather favour older drivers like Christopher because he was one of the white drivers who had been working in the cab office for a long time. When riders are going on a scheduled appointment or catching a train or plane, the delay caused by the cab office becomes problematic.

Our cab office was also a territory where drivers with racist tendencies felt comfortable enough to verbalise their narcissism. Some self-centred failed individuals who could not recognise their own ineptness and saw others as the reason for their failure. I remember the day when I was next to go and it was an off-peak hour, a very quiet period. There was a booked trip to Heathrow Airport which I was hoping to get. Five minutes before the Heathrow airport job, the controller gave me another booked trip. I was not happy but the trip offered to me was a long distance job also. I arrived at my pick-up address, the entrance of a tower building, with no way to knock on the door because of the height of the building. I could only rely on the controller to call the rider and inform them about their cab's position. After twenty minutes waiting to no avail, I returned to base on the controller's request, and as expected, I was fuming. I had no doubt it was a deliberate error to pass the airport job to another driver who happened to be the controller's friend. I was mad at the controller, shouting and telling him off for his malicious behaviour. The other white drivers, who believed it was their duty to defend one of their own, became defensive. They waded in and started to call me derogatory names. One of them said:

'If you don't like it here … you know what to do.'

Another even stood as an alibi.

'I was in the office when the controller received that trip,' he said.

'I knocked on the rider's door and she said she did not call a cab,' I replied. They all went quiet because they believed I had spoken to the resident at the address. It clarified my suspicion that the trip been fabricated to prioritise the controller's friend over me. The controller was a gambler and even though he got paid every Friday, by Monday he needed money to quench his addiction. Horse racing was the gambling addiction most white drivers, including the controller, had. The slogan "If you don't like it here … you know what to do" is very racist and was regularly used in the cab office by white drivers. It was mostly used when native African drivers complained about foul play by the controller. Their vague entitlement allowed the racists to tell us to suck it or go back where we come from. I witnessed how organised they were when defending the controller who was supposed to dispatch jobs in a chronological order and not to favour some. The only reason I was in Walworth Road every day was to earn a pound note and every time I was unfairly refused a trip, it was very annoying. While I was waiting for the trip that never materialised, I figured out how to trap the controller. I didn't speak to the rider. I was nowhere near his address. That behaviour was a regular occurrence at our cab office but it was difficult to prove it. I'm a character who never lies back when someone plays dirty on me; I was always looking at what to do about the situation.

The cab office was on a road where car boot sales were held every Sunday. I bought a hand bell with the intention of using it for fun somehow. One Friday morning, I was given three consecutive trips that were all no shows. I was very cross with the controller but I wasn't sure if it was deliberate because it was quite busy. I took a hastened decision on my way back to the cab office to demonstrate my frustration. I rang the bell inside the controller's little office continuously until it drove him completely mad. To calm me down, he gave me an airport wait and return booked trip. Even though I made a lot of money out of that job, it opened the door for a new game. Every time he favoured his chum over me, I'd spend my waiting time ringing the bell until I was given a trip. I also used the bell to interrupt racist conversation when idleness from a quiet period gave the white drivers a subject of discourse on African matters. However, he gave me the nickname of Jaws, likening me to the killer shark of Steven Spielberg's blockbuster film. He was always happy when I wasn't in the office, meaning I was more on the road and earning.

There has never been a time in my life where I've had a break from oppression. Neo-colonialism in the African continent was a continuity of colonialism which was also the continuation of slavery. Although the white drivers I worked with were the least privileged of their community, they felt they had better living conditions than me. Most of them could not read or write; they got most of their ideas about world views from the headline of the tabloid newspaper. Generally, their sources of information were biased and opinionated, and far from reality. A driver asked me one day where people sleep at night with all those wild animals about. I understood where he got the idea from because most African holidays adverts are pictures from the safari park. I had a good answer for him.

'We humans, are part of the animal family,' I told him. 'The animals know that too, and we're safer with them than our fellow humans. They don't enslave, colonise or oppress other animals. They kill to feed themselves … unlike we humans who killed for fun, greed and influence,' I replied.

The sense of belonging meant they could say what they wanted without being reprimanded. They picked and chose trips from African riders whom they deemed inadequate, just because of the colour of their skin. Mimicking the

African accent was the game of one particular driver who, for some unknown reason, continually thought it was funny. On that particular day, a rider, who was a female native African from Nigeria, walked into the cab office and requested a ride. She was going to Woodford which is in east London but the controller thought she meant Woodford House, a building situated on Portland Street near the cab office. She was given a quote of four pounds which, at the time, was a minimum fare. The trip was allocated to the driver with the mimicking attitude. Ten minutes later, he returned to the cab office with the rider. He'd left her in his cab, come into the cab office and turned to the controller.

'Where did she say she was going?' he asked.

'Woodford House,' replied the controller.

'I took her there and she looked at the building as if she was lost. *I told the controller I'm going to Woodford.*' (Repeating the conversation of his rider with a strange Nigerian accent.) 'I told her the trip was quoted at four pounds because she'd told the controller Portland Street. There's no way he would quote that price if he knew you were going to Woodford,' he told the controller.

Then the rider walked into the cab office and addressed the controller in her strong West African accent.

'Why is this driver wasting my time? I told him even though there was a misunderstanding between the controller and I, he should take me to Woodford and whatever the price I will pay. He just drove back straight to the cab office,' she told the controller.

The driver replied to her with his strange West African accent.

'You did not say whatever the price you'll pay. I will take you there if you pay the right fare of twenty-five pounds.'

I sat next to him, listening to him mocking but thought he was joking. He had one strange African name which he used to call every African driver in the cab office. I put up with his behaviour just because I was tired of fighting narcissism.

One thing that white drivers in our office did every morning was to buy a newspaper. Their two most popular brands were the *Daily Mail* and *The Sun*. These two are the biggest selling newspapers in England, and they are also known for their editorial views. They shout fire when there's none. They regularly run stories that spread fear in their readers about migrants and that leads to resentment. My white colleagues didn't just buy these newspapers for the current events, especially because they only read the headline as most of them had never read a full column. It was to help them with the horse racing analysis and to guide them on decisions for their gambling habits. I used to avail myself on their abandoned newspaper to read the columns. I wanted to understand how these privately educated scholars managed to convince their ill-informed readers to see we migrants as the cause of their problems. After reading a lot of editions, I became less angry with the drivers with racist tendencies. If, in Cameroon, a newspaper was continuously writing these types of opinionated ideas about Arabs and Europeans, I could have grown up with a resentful mindset. I may be hating innocent individuals who have meant no harm to me personally. I was in the cab office one afternoon with my mimicking colleague. It was very quiet. The controller was in the betting office even though he didn't have any money to bet.

'Nothing is going on is it?' I asked him.

'No one has any money left. Everyone is broke,' he replied.

'Not everyone, mate. There are many people with far better jobs out there who are not broke,' I said.

'This cab office was busier before you lot came and destroyed it,' he replied. 'If you are reduced to being a mini-cab driver in the country from where you claimed entitlement, with an education system that favoured you over other minority groups with a career opportunity designed to help people of your ilk, and you still manage to squander all these advantages ... you should be looking at yourself instead of thinking the black drivers and riders are the problems,' I told him.

He didn't reply but I knew that day he would go home and think about what I had said.

With time, the white driver became less vocally racist towards me. It happened after he realised that I treated his family members with respect in his absence. We were always arguing and at one stage I had a fight with him, trust me, I was a fighter. One day, his daughter came to the cab office after shopping so her father could drive her home. He was on a trip that took him over an hour; I was there to give her a lift free of charge. I did it because she was a family member of my colleague whatever our differences. From that day on, I was no more on his target list; I was exempt from his racist remarks. He knew Africa very well without ever stepping a foot in the continent. He also knew how people in Africa are violent and nasty to each other. The first time I encountered racism from one of these low lives, I was broken for a day or two, but I quickly realised that the way I felt was the only result the racist intended. He was less privileged and less educated than me, but his whiteness was more important to him as he felt calling me a "black bastard" and "monkey" satisfied his narcissistic views. The incident happened when I was working as a kitchen porter, washing up pots and plates with the man. We did our evening shift together and had a disagreement about who should be at the receiving end of the dishwasher. After that incident, I rose above my inferiority complex feelings and vouched to stand tall against any mental attack. Their badges of honour are an everlasting stain on their record, a criminal endorsement on their record, and it will haunt them all their life and reduce them only to jobs that need no formal check.

One Saturday, it was surprisingly busy very early in the day, and I was wondering why. Some white drivers were not accepting trips. When I returned to pick up a base rider, I realised why these drivers had suspended their daily earnings. Frankie Fraser was filming a documentary about his previous colourful life in a British traditional restaurant. The action was happening next to our cab office in a pie and mash restaurant. He dressed in a vintage English traditional costume and was using a prestigious British vintage car. He was in a Daimler limousine and there were three other prestigious vintage cars with some actors in them. I thought the old man was a Peer from the House of Lord. Passers-by, including my white colleagues, gathered around the scene in admiration. The controller later told me he was a professional gangster who had spent forty-two years in prison. I didn't understand why my colleagues were so passionate to see him and talked about him as though he was a role model. I later noticed that he moved nearby and was a regular rider of our cab service. I took him on trips many times to several destinations. He was simply an ordinary and friendly rider, just like other people of his age. However, his daughter, whose only qualification was being the daughter of Frankie Fraser, was a regular rider. The white drivers did not have a problem taking her, even though most of the time she did not have the means to pay. She was always high on drugs and the only time she was not high was when she was going to buy the illegal substance. Being the daughter of Frankie Fraser was not enough for me to drive her with the notion of not being paid at the end of the trip. I didn't care about the profession of her father; if she wanted my service, I always requested the fare up front. White drivers who often refused to drive black riders in fear of not being paid were comfortable with Frankie Fraser's daughter.

Drivers who were Licensed London Private-Hire Drivers had to have a clean criminal record. They also had to prove their fitness to drive strangers. Most of the white drivers could not satisfy the licensing authority's demands to be issued a licence. My colleagues had never been educated about the origins of the wealth that built the society they were born into. The exploitation of natural resources from around the world contributed to the industrial revolution which has given Britain a big advantage. Ignorance was the handicap which led them into a cul-de-sac. Rather than capitalising on the opportunities available to them, they concentrated on hating people that looked different to them. I still see some of my ex-colleagues around the public house while on a trip. One driver who I used to argue with all the time is now doing a painting and decorating job. If I was the one with a criminal record, I would not have a second chance, even if I retrained as a painter and decorator.

'Are you still doing the taxicab in the same area?' he asked me.

'Of course, what else can I do?' I replied.

'Get a life. I'm doing painting and decorating now and I'm very happy,' he said.

'Even if I retrained like you, I would not have the same opportunities like you. I'd rather stick with my cab career,' I replied.

Trust is the only thing that makes a difference between my white ex-colleague and I in the eyes of the client. I'll be judged by my appearance and not my ability to do the job. I know that trust has been my invisible barrier as I have witnessed on countless occasions during my career as a taxi driver. On many occasions, I have to prove I'm a trusted driver before gaining the confidence of my riders. In contrast, white riders trusted many convicted criminal white drivers just from their appearance. Many of them, I knew, should not be anywhere near the steering wheel of a taxicab. I had another white ex-colleague who was known for his vocal racist words. He became a window cleaner after failing to obtain a licence to drive a taxicab. A window cleaning job is somehow complicated because of the business premises that the workers have access into. Those businesspeople trust them to be inside their premises, hoping that they are all law-abiding citizens. However, if that sector was overrepresented by blacks, I have no doubt the businesspeople would've reacted differently.

EIGHT

THE LEGACY OF COLONIALISM

There were some familiar addresses from where I was always delighted to accept a request, because they were nice people who it was a pleasure to drive. I was given a job one afternoon to pick up a female rider who I knew at Lorrimore Road, South East 17. When I arrived at her address, she was waiting outside. She was looking four doors down her road at a woman and her two children who were going into the house. There were two men offloading house furniture from a van into the house. She boarded my cab with a reflexive mind.

'Hello, my brother, I can't believe those people are moving in this area, huh,' she told me.

'What's wrong with them?' I asked.

She clapped her hands.

'They are going to destroy my neighbourhood. They are very dirty,' she said.

The woman and her children had looked Somalian, Ethiopian or Eritrean.

'Have you had a friend from that community?' I asked her.

She said no.

'Have you known a colleague at work?' I asked her again.

She said no.

'Have you been to Ethiopia or flown with Ethiopian Airlines?' I asked her.

She said no.

I was very familiar with this rider, we usually have good, constructive conversation so I felt comfortable to speak plainly with her.

'How do you know so much about those people yet you have never had any social or business contact with them?' I asked her.

My rider was a native African from Nigeria, a country that shared colonial boundaries with Cameroon. Usually, we had a lot in common but on this subject we were miles apart.

'You know what I mean, my brother. These people are different, a bit backward. Their children are not well behaved,' she told me.

'I don't know the people from East Africa well enough to comment about their habits, but with some of them that I've come across, my experiences have always been positive,' I replied.

There was a silence between us for about five minutes. I understood what she was telling me because we were from a similar social and political construct. Our two countries share the same tribal problem, with so many different ethnic groups. We point at each other's differences the entire time and use one bad example to generalise the behaviour of the entire tribe. I know that if I have stepped on her toes, she will find something nasty about my country to identify me with. My rider and I were not born in Britain, nor in Europe;

we migrated here for economic reasons. Even though I did not have the opportunity to know whether the Ethiopian woman was born here, I assumed she had only migrated here, like us. In hindsight, the woman from Ethiopia, my rider and I should be considering a single tribe in the UK. What my rider was doing to her new neighbour was what migrants like us suffer in the hands of some white. Racist behaviours are driven by misleading information and my rider, without knowing her new neighbour, had formed her opinions from biased sources.

'We should not copy racist behaviour and use it against each other. By doing this to ourselves, it is a form of tribalism. We are too divided,' I told her.

People who act on their prejudiced tendencies hardly know their victims. My rider was unconsciously making that same mistake and the repercussions could hurt her severely in the future. It was a good thing that she wasn't travelling with her children on that trip. I hoped our conversations made her review her position. My job has given me the opportunity to create friendships amongst nearly every nationality in the world. I understand and accept that not everyone has the privilege to be close and personal to strangers the way my job has afforded me. The default human position to prejudge people before meeting them, as my rider did, is endemic.

East Street Market brought many riders into our pick-up zone. Being away from their address meant they relied on a shop name to indicate their pick-up location. The junction in which my rider was waiting had others waiting too. I didn't know who my rider was because the controller couldn't remember her name. On the cab radio, he told me to ask for the person who was going to Brixton. Coincidentally, there were two females heading in that direction – one black and the other white. I asked the controller if my rider was white or black and he told me she sounded like a black woman. I finally got my rider on board, and we set off.

'By the way, cab man, I'm not black as you referred to me,' she told me.

'I'm sorry, I should have referred to you as African,' I replied.

'Hell, not! I'm not African,' she told me.

'How should I have referred to you then, since I didn't know you?' I asked. 'Highly light,' she told me. She did have a very light skin.

There are many Africans who are lighter in complexion than she was who refer to themselves as black.

'I'm not from Africa, I was born and bred in the West Indies,' she continued. 'I meant African descent, regardless of your birthplace,' I replied.

'I'm not of African descent and I have no connection with the continent of Africa,' she said. 'By the way, my name is Angela Brown.'

'My name is Andrew Njanjo,' I told her.

'You have an African name and you have an African accent. You've the right to refer to yourself as black,' she replied.

My rider was very polite and was making her point in a respectful manner.

'Being African or black is not just where someone is born but rather where one's ancestors originated from,' I told her.

'You've got an African name, you know exactly which tribe you belong to in the African continent, I couldn't say that for myself,' she told me.

'Andrew is not an African name, but rather a reminder of the colonial movement,' I told her.

There was nothing I could tell my rider that could change her mind. The divide was not just within Africans living in the continent, it extended to those in the diaspora as well.

Near our cab office, there was a particular African shop, which sold African food. White drivers would not pick up from that shop because the riders' goods often included frozen fish. They were also known for booking their ride while still shopping, causing the driver to wait unnecessarily. One day, a rider waited for over thirty minutes until a driver who could accept the job arrived. I was the next driver who didn't refuse jobs from that shop. On our way to her destination, I was involved in a little road argument with another driver. London roads are very tight and road rage usually stems from sharing the narrow lanes. Two fully decorated Harley Davidson motorbikes would struggle to negotiate the way through some London roads. This incident happened on a two-way road for cars with designated parking spaces on both sides. The other driver had little Jamaican boxing gloves on his interior driving mirror. He was a black man, younger than me and spoke with an Afro-Caribbean accent. The argument was getting serious. My rider, who was already late from being delayed at the cab office, was blaming the other driver for not exercising a bit of patience. Although I had the right of way over the oncoming vehicle, as a cab driver, my time was precious, so I killed the argument by reversing and gave way to the other driver. As the other driver passed by, my rider was still angry at him and called him slave. I asked her not to use that word to describe anybody, especially native Africans.

'My brother, these people were slaves that we sold because we didn't want them,' she told me.

We have been miseducated about our own history so much that we're now using the slave traders' version of the dark moments of our past.

'If anybody is a slave, it's me. I was a slave in Africa and now I'm a slave in Britain and I can guarantee you that I will be a slave all my life,' I told her. 'I was doing jobs in Africa that even Africans who were forced into slavery would not do, and in Britain I have washed plates and cutlery in the kitchen as a day job, I have cleaned toilets and offices for bankers to work in a comfortable and clean environment. That man is probably working in that comfortable environment and you think he is a slave?' I asked her.

She was speechless because she thought I was going to back her on her narcissistic personality disorder. After I dropped her, I was hurt and disappointed. I've been protected by Africans born in the Caribbean more than Africans born in the continent. My girlfriend at the time was an African woman born in the Caribbean. Africans from the Caribbean have made a lot of sacrifices towards the freedom we newcomers benefit from today in Britain.

I was born and bred two hundred and fifty miles away from my tribal boundaries in Cameroon. I've faced tribalism from a young age and I've developed a coping mechanism to deal with it. I grew up with friends in my rural town in Mutengene, every time I did something wrong, people always associated my behaviour with my tribe of origin. At the time, I didn't even know how people in my tribe of origin behaved because I'd never lived there. My childhood friends were from tribes other than where we were born and bred, and they, too, suffered the same tribal dogma. Neighbours were so emotional in expressing their opinions by associating each and every one of our behaviours with our different tribes. Although we did something that was deemed not nice collectively, our influences were somehow from five different tribes. The prejudiced nature that we human are born with progressively leads to unconscious bias. I couldn't explain the situation to my parents because they also suffered from the same tribal remarks. Although I've not witnessed people saying it in front of them, they referred to them in association with their tribe even though they were the early settlers in the town. I learned to accept tribalism as part of life within my remit and refrain from complaining. When I faced racism in the United Kingdom, I used that same coping mechanism to face people with ignorant stereotypical views.

Growing up in southwest Cameroon, I was misled about the Rastafarian movement. I was repeatedly told they were mad people who spent their time smoking marijuana. However, everyone around were fans of the legendary Bob Marley, but never associated his Rastafarian beliefs with his music. When I came to live in London, I got a job at King's College Hospital as a kitchen porter. I met a colleague who was also a porter. Karl was an African born on the Caribbean island of Jamaica. One day, we finished at the same time and I saw his dreadlocks for the first time.

'Are you a Rastafarian?' I asked him. He smiled.

I was shocked because he was the opposite of everything I knew about Rastafarians. I was re-educated to differentiate between people who styled their hair with locks and Rastafarians. Karl was my first real history teacher. He knew more about Africa than most of us who were born and bred in the continent. He was the first man to educate me about the European Civil War. He was talking about what the Europeans called World War One and Two. He told me the Europeans were disputing invaded territory in the continent of Africa, and that Southwest Cameroon and Congo were the reasons why Germany was upset. Southwest Cameroon was occupied by Germany but they wanted Congo as well because of the minerals that generate tantalum. The Belgians did not agree and that created a disagreement between them. It makes a lot of sense to me because I was born in the Southwest region of Cameroon and before the First World War it was occupied by the Germans. The region only became a British-occupied territory after Britain and their allies defeated Germany in their civil war. During our one-hour break, we were having our lunch together.

'Have you ever been in Africa?' I asked him.

'Not yet, but I'm not just planning to go there for a holiday, but to settle there one day,' he replied.

'How do you know more about Africa than me?' I asked him.

'Bob Marley's inspirational ideologies did not come from mainland Africa. They came from the Maroons ... the home of Rasta. Andrew, I don't wear locks for fashion, I'm a Rastafarian,' he told me.

What I learned from Karl was not just the historical enlightenment of Africa, but the foundation of the divisions within each state. All the artificial boundaries did not respect the indigenous tribal boundaries, rather the interest of white invaders for the pursuit of material gain.

Airport trips can be boring or exciting, depending on the rider's mood. I picked up a native African passenger one day at around midday; he was going to Gatwick Airport. During the trip, we started a discussion common about African issues that we had encountered in the West.

'Where are you from?' he asked.

'I'm from Cameroon,' I told him.

He looked at me in dismay.

'No! You're not. You are from Nigeria,' he told me.

'What makes you think I'm from Nigeria?' I asked him.

'You look like a Nigerian. More like an Igbo man … even your accent sounds Igbo,' he told me.

I grew up in the rural town of Mutengene which has many families from the Nigerian tribe of Igbo. One of my best friend's parents was Igbo but he was born and bred in the same town as me. Our friendship brought our parents closer. Whenever we were late returning home, both sets of parents thought we were in one house or the other. Telling me I looked and sounded like people from that tribe was a bonus to me. 'Nigeria is bigger and richer than Cameroon. What benefit would I get from saying I am from a country inferior to my own?' I asked him.

'A Nigerian citizen can travel to Cameroon to acquire a Cameroon passport which can facilitate the visa process for European and American destinations,' he told me.

'Are you from Nigeria? You seem to know the people from there so well,' I asked.

'I'm from Cameroon,' he told me.

'Which part of Cameroon are you from?' I asked him.

'The southwest, Mutengene is my hometown,' he told me.

Mutengene is where I was born and bred and I know

every family who were there at the time I was there until I travelled to live in Cameroon's biggest city of Douala.

'I was born and bred in Mutengene,' I told him.

'You're joking, right? What is your family name?' he asked me.

'Djomo!' I replied.

He looked at me in surprise.

'Do you know Jean Djomo?' he asked me.

I laughed.

'I went to school with him. We're still in touch every time I visit Cameroon,' he told me.

'What's your family name?' I asked him.

'Nyemti,' he told me.

'I grew up with Okouh and Ashu Nyemti. Mr Nyemti was the president of Top Tarzan,' I told him.

I was travelling with a rider I had grown up with, but difficult conditions had separated our paths. A week later, I received a call from a relative who was still living in Mutengene. He told me he was with Omoh, the passenger I had taken to the airport. My rider originated from the southwest province. His tribal boundaries were divided into two by colonial invaders when they were partitioning their exploited territories. One side of his tribe was in Nigeria while the other was in French Cameroon. That's how many native Africans see the differences between themselves more than their similarities. The collective strength has been taken away by the colonial invasion and Africans have more in common with their colonial masters than their fellow Africans.

NINE

Driving a taxicab in London means transporting people whatever their race, gender, sexual orientation and disability. I grew up in a country where none of the LGBTQ (Lesbian, Gay, Bisexual, Transgender and Queer) community existed. Perhaps, some people were homosexual, but I was never aware of it, and it wasn't something I really thought of growing up. However, religions was one of the few places where part of their teaching was homosexual relations. I grew up with the knowledge that most teachings in theology were far alienated from human experience. In Cameroon, homosexuality was and still is against the law. However, the problem is not the enforcement because things move very slowly in the investigation department. The country has a population that does not respect the human rights law. A homosexual would be safer in the hands of the authorities than facing mob justice from a population who react with their emotions. My first experience driving a member of this minority group was a rider whose name was Jo. The long version of the name could be Joseph for a male or Josephine for a female. When I picked up my rider, she was a female but when she spoke to me concerning her journey, she had a strong male sounding voice. I became curious, looking at her again, hoping to find something that would confirm my suspicion. She noticed I was gazing at her through my internal driving mirror as our eyes met several times. She was a fully transgender female. I was surprised she wasn't concerned about me glancing at her, but she just wanted to get to her destination. She did not give me any problem and she paid her fare accordingly. I don't normally think of my riders after I have finished a trip, but as my first transgender experience, I remembered it for a long time. In Cameroon, even if you feel trapped in the wrong body as many transgender people would explain, many people do not have enough money to pay for their regular medical bill let alone finance the transition process. There was a driver in our cab office who was overtly proud of his strong Christian beliefs. He was always measuring everything he did to be in accordance with religious teachings. One day, he picked up two riders who happened to be a homosexual couple. They sat next to each other and, overhearing their conversation, he concluded that they were gay. He stopped his cab and threw them out. The riders did complain to the cab office but it led to no action against the driver. At the time, there was no law preventing cab drivers withdrawing their services for discriminatory reasons. The first time I noticed a gay couple in my cab was when I picked up two male riders who sat close to each other. Normally when two passengers decide to sit in the back, it's usually for their business or a private conversation. Usually, they would sit on the outer seats, leaving the middle one empty. Even when I carry heterosexual couples, they hardly ever sit tightly together except when they are coming from a party.

However, my heterosexual couple were not just sitting close to each other but they were holding hands, thus leaving me with only one conclusion about themselves. For a cab driver who was born and bred in the United Kingdom, it would be just another couple who have chosen their lifestyle. For me, it was strange because I had never been exposed to people with different sexual desires to me. Even though they did not mean to provoke any reaction from me, I felt as if they were trying to let me know who they were.

Working at night was never my thing. A friend told me that I could earn more than twice as much as usual on a Friday and Saturday night at the Fridge nightclub in Brixton. All they required there was my private-hire insurance and the rent of £40 for both nights. When I arrived at the club, I was amazed that the rent fee was paid to a bouncer with a high-visibility jacket and a clipboard. I thought they were operating an illegal cab office because at the time the mini-cab trade was not licensed. Little did I know it was a gay nightclub, not that it bothered me when I realised. I was more concerned about my turnover. It was the first time I had worked from a nightclub that was exclusively homosexual. The difference between gay nightclub riders and those from a heterosexual nightclub was the turnover. I picked up a rider who lived fifty miles away from London and he didn't haggle about the amount I charged him. During the trip, he was very quiet and just wanted to reach his destination. Michael Barrymore was a regular guest at the club. When he wanted to go home, the driver next on the queue would have a weekend fulfilled due to his generosity. The only incident I had during my time working there was with a passenger who was escorted out of the club by the security. He was thrown out for reasons unknown to we drivers waiting for a fare. It was my turn in the queue; he was going just five miles away. During the trip, he talked to himself until we arrived at his destination. When I told him the price, he thought I was overcharging him.

'It costs me ten pounds from my house to Brixton. How come the fare is double on return?' he asked me.

'The club has their own prices which are different from local cab offices,' I told him.

He looked at me in despair and gave me twenty pounds. Leaving the cab, he then slammed the cab door very hard in anger. I expected nothing less from a rider who had already had a problem before boarding my cab and having to pay a higher fare when his enjoyment was cut short. At the time, I'd just bought my cab and I was still in the honeymoon period with my investment. I was angry at my rider and was tempted to call him a derogatory name, often used to describe homosexuals, but I quickly stopped myself. I reminded myself of the majority of the very good passengers whom I've taken on several trips without issues instead, and have been highly rewarded by their generosity. My friend who introduced me to that nightclub did not mislead me on the high turnover, although he did not warn me that I'd be picking up riders with a completely different sexual orientation from me.

Soon after the private-hire trade was regulated, our cab office had a contract with a gay nightclub, the Crash nightclub in Vauxhall. A controller from our cab office was dispatching the jobs at the door of the club. Although she had a high-visibility jacket like most nightclubs, on this occasion the cab office's name was written on the back, letting the guests know that the service they were using was authentic. My advantage was that my cab office rent covered the trip taken at the nightclub. Although the controller quoted the fare, the price guide of the club trips was higher compared to the price for the same trip from the cab office. So, whenever a rider did not ask for a quote from the side controller but from the driver, it was like hitting the jackpot; a carte blanche to hike the price. We took advantage of the club members who wanted to go home as the nightclubs formally ran until early morning. Some of their dress designs were only appropriate for that territory. Most riders from the Crash nightclub were similar to those at the Fridge. Their journeys were long journeys and there were hardly any arguments about payment. The only time I had a little difficulty was with a rider who remembered, when he got to his destination, that he didn't have enough money for the fare. He slept in the back of the cab and forgot to withdraw money from an ATM, so he asked me to take him to the nearest cashpoint. Amazingly, he could not remember his personal identification number, and I was left with accepting five packets of Benson and Hedges as my option of payment. He went into the nearest shop and bought cigarettes; at the time, credit card payment required only an identical signature to the one on the back of the card. I was a smoker back then and accepting the packets of cigarettes in exchange for the fare was better than having no payment at all. Having this close contact with my homosexual rider eliminated the entire subconscious stigma that I had towards this marginalised group.

One morning, around 7 a.m., I took a gay couple, as the last job from the club hitting a traffic jam at Old Kent Road, I realised that nearly everybody was looking at my cab and smiling. I thought maybe my car was dirty or someone had thrown up on it. Looking in my rear-view mirror, I could see that the two guys were kissing each other and with great passion. If I could've hidden under the steering wheel and driven off, I would've done so. Although the passers-by were not looking at me, I still felt embarrassed because I was unconsciously having the same reaction as them. It was the first time I had experienced the true undercurrent of stereotypical feeling I had for homosexuals. I do not know why it took other people's reactions to intrigue the subconscious bias I've carried all along. Before that morning, I had transported many gay peoples without a second thought. The scenario in the back of my cab was not the first; it happened regularly. The journey usually happened at nighttime when the road traffic was usually fluid and fewer people were looking at travelling vehicles. I grew up in Cameroon with laws that criminalised homosexuality. Which has unequivocally informed my subconscious mind that homosexuality is a crime. When I noticed onlookers carrying thoughts similar to my previously held view, I joined them in reacting to their prejudiced views. I temporarily thought they might think I was a member of their community because we were sharing the same moving space. At no time did I feel unsafe while doing my job at the nightclub. In reality, gay people can tell the difference between a homosexual and a heterosexual. All along, I was completely removed from reality because my reason for going to that club was to earn a living. Most of my fellow drivers who were plying for fares at the nightclub were happy to drive homosexual people. We were there to earn a living, not to be judgemental about their activities. Of course, we may have sometimes joked about some of their kinky attire but that's who they were and we did so with no offence. In twenty-five years of doing this job, I have never had violence, racist comments or unfounded allegations from homosexual riders. If I hadn't been a cab driver and hadn't worked specifically at a gay nightclub, I would never have known about the level of my unconscious bias towards this minority group. I have picked up gay people from all walks of life; company directors, police officers, medical doctors, barristers. In reality, there's no profession in the world that is excluded from the LGBTQ community. As a mini-cab driver, even when my riders are not having a conversation with me but rather to themselves, I still pay close attention to their discussion. I do this with every passenger, mostly at night. I don't transport people for fun and sometimes their conversation can help me define their intention. By listening to riders, I can anticipate an intention to not pay me at the end of the journey. They may be going after a gang for the purpose of confrontation or other criminal engagement that may put me in danger. I grew up as an able bodied, heterosexual man in Cameroon. All the laws which governed the country favoured me. My position prevented me from knowing the struggle oppressed people really encounter. I wasn't aware of the struggle that women from my family and community were going through. I was brought up to be the dominant male contrary to the females in my family. Only when I arrived in the United Kingdom did I start to live on oppressed Struggle Street.

In 2005, I moved to a new flat in Bermondsey with my family. At the time, the far-right parade was taking place yearly and my flat was located on the route of the demonstration. During that period, I wasn't worrying just about my safety, but that of my family as a whole. The dominant character that I was in Cameroon became the target of some white dominant male in Britain. I started to understand how oppression can have a detrimental effect on people's everyday lives. I had to adopt a conscious mind not to be part of the problem of other oppressed minorities. Until everyone's human rights are protected, no one is protected because politician's views are always shifting. With the rise of populist movements around the world, opportunist politicians will interpret the human right law regionally to attract their followers. Before venturing into politics, Boris Johnson (PM) was a columnist on a newspaper. He used his platform to fuel racism on marginalised groups he knew nothing about. In his political career, he continued with the same ideology. During the European championships, the English team decided to take the knee in respect for the racial equality movement. The English football supporters, as every group of people do, had some difficult members who decided to boycott. A senior cabinet member whose job is supposed to be leading from the front to ensure equality instead protected the right of the racists to boo those taking the knee. However, the success of the team brought the country together when they reached the final but lost in a penalty shoot-out. In every case, losing a final at a football cup has always been upsetting and many supporters accept the result and move on. On this occasion, the racist supporters decided to direct their anger toward the black players with racist remarks. Prime Minister Johnson took to the stage to condemn the racists, even though he was part of their making, a change of heart from someone who was scared of losing his popularity. That's one reason politicians should never be given the opportunity to play politics with human rights laws.

Most of the drivers from our office who preferred to queue at the gay nightclub for fares were Africans. It was more productive than working at the cab office. We did not work there for any other reason. There was an incident which happened where a black gay man was being harassed by a group of four white gay men. They all came out of the nightclub and were having a heated argument which was nearly becoming physical. We all rushed towards the scene to make sure that the black man was not in any danger and we managed to defuse the situation. Being a native African, he lived as a disadvantaged minority in the United Kingdom. Being gay, his disadvantages doubled. In the cab queue I was the next driver. After that incident, I took that rider to Brighton. It was a long way and during the trip he fell asleep. Just as I was leaving the motorway, he woke up and gave me directions to his precise location. That created an exchange between us.

'Where're you from?' he asked me.

I guessed that he wanted to know my country of origin.

'Cameroon,' I replied.

'What's his name again? … Roger Miller … 1990 World Cup final in Italy.'

He cited before telling me where he originated from.

'I was born here but my parents are from Kenya,' he told me.

During our conversation, he explained the overwhelming support his parents, who never follow football, had for the Cameroon national team.

'I was ten years old at the time of that tournament and it turned him into a football fan,' he continued.

He was surprised why, up to date, an African country has not yet won a World Cup. He believed France was robbing the continent of their talent.

He said to me, 'France's World Cup triumph in 1998 was due to African players. I'm confident that an African country will lift the prestigious trophy in our lifetime.'

'I'm not sure about that. Pre-eminent African footballers see themselves playing for European countries rather than representing their nation,' I told him.

'Why is that? It's an honour to represent your country of origin,' he said.

'I'm sure African youths dream of representing their country. Their reasons for choosing their adoptive country over their country of origin rest with the football association of their respective countries,' I told him.

Being born and bred in the United Kingdom gave him an artificial view of African affairs. He was mistaking the European ways of running society with the way Africans managed their continent. At his destination, he was very generous with the fare he had been quoted, giving me twenty pound extra. On my way back to the nightclub in search for another trip, I carried the memory of the conversation we had had. I completely forgot that he was a gay man who had had problems at the nightclub. Although we had completely opposite sexual preferences, our commonalities and our interests were enormous.

As public hire law became effective, discrimination was no more accepted at every level, and the riders became aware of their rights. Taking into account the sector, there is a high percentage of religious drivers from different parts of the world. During Gay Pride, my trips are mainly from people of the LGBTQ community and sympathisers who are helping them celebrate in solidarity. One question that I was frequently asked by my gay riders was what did I think about the LGBTQ community? I had only one answer for them – live and let live. I guess they asked me because I'm black. I picked up riders who dressed in a drag queen costume during daytime and I didn't feel any way as I previously did. I've gone past my unconscious bias; I live under the jurisdiction of the laws laid down by a government chosen by the people in a democratic way. The LGBTQ community exists and has existed for a very long time, and they are here to stay. Because it is not part of my culture, doesn't mean that I must have a negative feeling about. I have a duty to educate my children not to carry any negative feeling about people they know nothing about them. Arming my children with hate for any set of people because of their differences can lead them into having a criminal mindset. I once picked up a rider, a white male who was not religious, but he was upset that the homosexuality agenda was forced onto children.

'My worry is that one of my children can grow up and be gay,' he told me.

'If one of your children becomes a drug addict, alcoholic or addicted to gambling, it doesn't make you a bad parent. You did not educate them that way,' I replied.

No one educates their children towards things that they do not conform to, but no one can pre-empt what the future will bring for their offspring. Every human being is born with their unique DNA and their desire and preferences are personal choices that the individual can comfortably make.

'I'm not worried about my children growing up in a country where the LGBTQ are free to express their desires, my biggest worry is the criminal sexual paedophile, whether they are heterosexual or homosexual,' I told him.

Our service had a regular rider who lived near our cab office with her parents. The female rider was in love with a persistent criminal who was in and out of prison regularly. I could see the detrimental effect on the woman every time I drove her to visit her boyfriend in prison.

'He promised to change his ways so we can spend quality time together but … every time he is released from prison, two months later he is back there,' she told me.

Even her parents, whom I also knew, were stressed about their daughter's choice but could not persuade her to let go of that infamous relationship. I wasn't aware of their family conversation about it all, but it was her personal choice and only she knew why she was attracted to him.

TEN

WITNESSING THE GROOMING PROCESS

The most difficult and sensitive part of my job is accepting trips from unaccompanied young people. The children of this modernity do not look their age. Shop assistants are required to ask for proof of identification to sell alcohol and cigarettes. Taxi drivers can only use their discretion and withdraw their service if they think their passenger needs to be accompanied. There are three common issues I have encountered: the responsibility of their well-being, their safety and getting paid at the end of the journey. They are not likely to be in employment and have been known to be problematic with fare settlement. When I was their age, paying a taxi driver at the end of my trip was like throwing away my money. The fare for me would've been better served to buy chocolate and sweets. I accepted a trip given during rush hour, a busy time for us. My rider was young, between the age of fifteen and seventeen years old. I knew, at that age, the whole world meant nothing as long as the attention was on them. During the trip, he asked me to stop on three occasions and spent a minimum of ten minutes on each stop. I began to worry because the waiting time was significantly increasing the fare. Collecting fare from these young people is challenging let alone the increased stoppage charges.

'The initial quote given at the beginning of the trip has increased to twelve pounds,' I told my young rider.

'Why is that? The controller told me six pounds. That's all I've got,' he replied.

I radioed the controller and explained all the stops and the duration of the journey. We both listened to the controller's voice on the radio. 'The three stops have now increased the fare to twelve pounds.' From then on, he started mimicking my accent to put his point across. I asked why he was using a different accent when speaking to me. He just repeated the question I had asked, mimicking my accent again. The young man was darker in skin complexion than me, and before the fare adjustments, he had spoken with a pure London accent. I found it strange for an African child to think my accent was funny or was alien to him. I wasn't angry with him, instead I saw a victim, a lost African prince. The geographical location he'd been brought up in had cast a cloud over his identity. His nationality had created an invincible barrier between him and I. I will be turning in my grave if one of my grand or even great grandchildren behaves like this towards an African. Children are creatures of their environment and this behaviour happened in my household. My children used my African accent between them to explain the way I react to certain situations. I've also witnessed them sometimes doing it as humour, but I've always intervened to let them know that it can never be used mischievously. After that, I drove the young man to his destination and didn't bother to insist on the increased waiting fare. I was trying to figure out how I could connect with this young man about our similarities.

'I was born in Cameroon,' I told my rider.

He looked at me and shrugged his shoulder.

'I migrated here in search for a better life. When I was your age, growing up on the street, I struggled like you can never imagine,' I said.

He slowly turned towards me and I sensed he wanted to know more.

'When I arrived here, I saw the opportunity you guys have. I wish I'd had it back home,' I continued.

'What opportunity? What do you know? You'll never understand what we're going through,' he replied.

'At least you have free education, free healthcare, you don't skip meals. Many children back home would bite off your hands just to have that,' I told him. 'My mum was born and bred in Ghana and she told me stories like that countless times,' he told me.

'I'm sure she wanted you to know where you come from. I do the same to my children,' I said.

Shortly afterwards, we arrived at his destination.

'Uncle … what's the fare?' he asked me.

'Six pounds,' I replied.

He gave me the exact money.

'Respect, uncle,' he said.

'Have a wonderful day,' I told him.

From that day, every time that young man saw me, he referred to me as uncle.

My rider should be proud of his Britishness and at the same time celebrate his African connection. He could be a force for good if he embraced both of the qualities that he had inherited. It's very important for the British-born African to learn their history and at the same time be proud of their British culture. They are inheriting a multi racial-cultural world. My young rider was not the first teenager who behaved in that way. I've had countless experiences but they usually behave like that to impress their peers who they are sharing the cab with. I picked up three teenagers once from the Heygate Estate. During the trip, one of them was behaving like a gang leader. He was clearly a bully just by the way he was talking to his peers. It got to the stage where I thought if I didn't intervene, it might get physical. I attempted to defuse the situation by reasoning with them positively. One of the teenagers had a strong west African accent and he was the one that the bully was picking on. He was trying to fit into the caricature behaviour of his peers but the bully was mocking his accent mischievously. The two sat in the back of my cab and their friend, who was older, sat in front. I kept looking in the rear-view mirror to check their behaviour. On several occasions, our eyes met and the bully noticed that I was paying attention to him and what he was doing.

'Are you alright, cabbie?' he asked me. I nodded.

I used that opportunity to tell him what I'd been thinking about his behaviour.

'You know, the English language has got many accents. There's no need to mock your friend because of his accent,' I told him.

'Focus on your driving, cab man. You may crash 'cause you're too concerned about what I'm doing which is none of your business,' he replied.

'If you want to bully your friend, please do it after your trip. I won't tolerate it in my cab, young man,' I told him.

The rider in the front seat who looked older than the two others turned to them, speaking their street language.

'Allow him,' he told the bully.

Calm was restored and, on that occasion, my contribution was negatively received by the bully. It created the opposite effect to what I intended. I could not reason with them in that situation because it was escalating the behaviour of the bully. He wanted to prove how bold he was. My intention was not only to change their attitude, as some of them have already reached a point of no return. I did it to appease the situation. However, on the occasion of my teenage rider, I managed to reason with the young mind who was at the beginning of derailment.

There are young people who are used as dispatchers for drug lords. The henchmen use our cab service to collect money from the rats, or soldiers, as they refer to them. I took this YOUTH, that's how they refer to the younger soldiers in my ENDS, meaning my territory. He was between fourteen to fifteen years old. He dressed very smartly with designer jeans, a name-brand T-shirt and Nike training shoes. However, he forgot to buy a designer belt to keep his trousers up.

'Yoh,' cabbie. Burst left … yeah, burst right … wait here!' he ordered me.

He was giving me directions though he knew I knew how to get to his destination. He wanted to be in control and his choice of route was for a reason known to him alone. He left my cab and walked towards a white male, they had a brief exchange and then he came back. On to the next destination. While he was giving me directions, he was also on the phone, taking directions. Obviously, he was selling drugs and he knew I knew what he was doing. He also knew

I would never inform the police about his activities. At the end of the ride, he removed a packet of banknotes and paid the bare minimum. On that occasion, I was short paid, but I wasn't worried about the amount of money he had in his possession as I knew it was not his money. Later on the same day, I picked up an older drug dealer. His trip was booked at the cab office as AD (as directed). He sat in the back seat and was continuously on the phone throughout the journey. He was well dressed in name-brand clothing, wearing dark designer sunglasses and he had his single-use cup of coffee. I knew he was going around collecting money from the youths and supplying them with some more drugs to dispatch. He ignored my presence while he engaged in a phone conversation that was quite clearly exposing his business. He did not care if I was listening to his conversation because he knew there was nothing I could do about the information. He knew where I worked and he knew I was out to hustle behind the wheel and I was not a Crimestoppers agent. That was all I knew of his illegal activity. Where the drugs were coming from or where the money was going, I didn't know. The young man, also called a foot soldier, who actually sold the drugs, was a teenager of school age and should have been at school.

Driving in the same pick-up area exposed me to how teenagers end up dealing drugs, a business that is the most dangerous in the world in a lawless environment. I witnessed the process of a teenager being recruited. It happened around a local fried chicken shop. It sounds incredible to think that offering a young mind a chicken meal worth £3.99 can turn him into a drugs slave. It was a drip drip process. Veteran drug dealers don't like to distribute the illegal substances themselves because they are known by the police. Instead, they try to recruit as many innocent juveniles as they can to do this for them. I accepted a request from an older drug dealer on a round trip. He stopped near a fried chicken shop and walked towards a teenager. There were lots of school people around who had just finished school for the day. They had a little exchange as though they were family. I knew they were not family just by analysing their body language. After a short exchange with the teenager, he offered a banknote to him. The teenager hesitated to accept the money, and he had to insist several times before the boy took it. I watched from a distance but when he approached my cab again, I pretended I had been concentrating on my phone all along. He targeted that teenager because he usually roamed the street long after school. There was no one to go home to. By transporting the older drug dealer around the area, I generated more information about the grooming process. The older dealer was slowly becoming a role model, a protective person for the teenager, occupying the position of the father. Working in the area for a long time, I knew the teenager's mother who was a single parent. On one occasion during a trip, he stopped at the teenager's school at closing time and asked me to wait.

'I'm picking up my nephew. Let's wait here,' he said.

I knew he was telling a fib. On our way back with the teenager, in the back of my cab, he gave him a gift in a carrier bag. The teenager was not excited because he didn't know what was inside.

He told him, 'I got you the Nike Air you've always wanted.'

The teenager looked into the carrier bag, with a little smile.

'Thank you,' he said.

At no point during the trip did the teenager refer to him as uncle or cousin. It confirmed my suspicions that they were not family.

I knew the mother of the teenager from taking her on trips many times. She was one of the best mothers anyone could wish for. She was a single mother and the breadwinner of the family, and like many other Africans living in London, did not have the family base support. If she was in her homeland, the teenager would have gone to stay with his cousins after school until his mother finished work. The drug dealer filled that gap until his mother returned from work, but to his own benefit. Not long afterwards, the teenager started to dress in expensive footwear and clothes. I accepted a request from the teenager and I noticed a change of attitude. He was behaving like he didn't know me and was always on his mobile phone. His conversation was about a sports car that he intended to buy. However, at no point during his conversation did he mention taking a driving lesson. Although we shared the same confined space in the moving vehicle, he was doing everything to avoid engaging with me verbally or physically. He was physically in my cab but his presence was absent. His new world of false hopes and invisible danger had taken precedence. The older drug dealer's job was done and from then on, I regarded the teenager and his mentor drug dealer as people I should not cross paths with.

Life in London is very expensive, and single parents are usually at the bottom of the breadline. I was on a trip with the mother of the teenager one Saturday afternoon. She was going to the wedding ceremony of a work colleague. It was a long trip and the London traffic made the journey even longer. During the trip, we spoke about many things without mentioning her son. I was reluctant to talk about her teenager because I didn't know what she thought of his new life. Halfway through the trip, she mentioned the changes in her son's situation.

'My boy doesn't go to school anymore,' she told me.

I pretended not to know.

'Oh no! How come?' I asked her.

'He has become a businessman. I tried to convince him otherwise but you know how money can alter one's attitude,' she said.

'Wow! That's great. What line of business is he in?' I asked.

I sensed that she was naïve about the activities of her teenager.

'He is affiliated to a group that runs tickets for ... What did he call it? ... ticket touting,' she replied.

'For events?' I asked.

'There are many ways to make money if you know what you're doing in this country,' she continued.

I was tempted to let her know that her child was in danger but was reluctant because of the repercussions. If the teenager knew I had told his mother about his activities, my life could be in danger. I also didn't want to disappoint her when she thought his financial contribution on the running of the household was a bonus.

'I'm in the wrong job. After so many years driving a taxi, I still struggle with my bills,' I told her.

'My boy is a big man now. He contributes to the house like a partner ... at least I can benefit from his little business,' she said.

She was attending a happy ceremony and it would not be the last time I'd see her. I knew we would have another opportunity to discuss this further.

A year later, I was on a ride with the teenager's mother, and by then she was aware of her son's activities. Our conversation was somehow different because her son was now known by the authorities.

'The name-brand clothes and shoes of my boy were not funded by his ticket touting business,' she told me.

It was little too late, the ship had sailed. The boy was already a criminal.

'The police came to my house. They searched my flat as if I was a criminal,' she told me.

'Do they think you are a fraudster or what?' I asked her.

'According to them, my son is suspected of carrying drugs for the purpose of distribution,' she told me.

'Wow! That's serious. Is he selling drugs?' I asked.

'I don't know. I spend all my day at work, I don't know what to think,' she replied.

I knew she was aware of her son activities. She was in a catch twenty-two; her teenager would rebel against her if challenged. He would be hunted by the older dealer if he disobeyed the order to dispatch his drugs. She asked me if I knew about her son's illegal activities. I told her I work on the road, day in day out, but my rider's activities are none of my business. Her son was already in trouble with the police and would definitely spend time in prison, and my rider knew that.

There are many mothers whose children have been caught in this situation and they have found a way to intervene and steer them back on the right track. A mother whom I regularly took on a trip once told me the story of her son which was similar to this. The only way she solved the problem was to send her teenager to a boarding school in Ghana. The man returned after his A-levels and was a different person. He achieved a first-class degree at university, got a high-earning job and became a respectable citizen. Once in Ghana, he realised the opportunities he had in Britain. He also discovered who he really was. The experience prompted him to work hard at college and he took advantage of his opportunities in the UK on his return. I also regularly picked up a single mother who happened to be a devoted Christian. She referred to herself as a born-again Christian. She told me a born-again Christian was spiritually superior to ordinary Christians. She had three boys whom she brought up in a strict religious manner. The boys were never in trouble and did not hang around with the streetwise.

'I pray twice a day for my boys to be guided by the Holy Ghost,' she told me. 'I communicate to my children through my traditional language more often than in English … so they never forget where they are from,' she continued.

Her trip was a twenty minute drive and I learned much about her strategy.

'Your professional career was also a factor of your boys' success. Parents who lead by example are likely to guide their children in the right path of life,' I replied.

She was a midwife.

'The sermon in the church is aimed at every person … and everybody will analyse it from their own experience,' I told her.

My suggestion prompted her to explain her deep conviction about her being born again.

'When I found the right church that delivered the word of God the right way and at me especially, I knew my life and those around me would never be the same,' she told me. 'I spend forty to fifty hours a week at work. The upbringing of my children is a full time job. You're a taxi driver … I won't lecture you about the behaviour of the children in this country,' she continued.

I was lost for words because everything she said made no sense to me.

'Your professional career creates a more realistic life around your children. It has created positivity and aspirations in the family setting,' I replied.

This was what I thought about my rider's strategy but the summary of our discourse was that her belief in God was paramount.

'Before you became religious or a born-again Christian, you were already a good person,' I said.

My education as a human being began when I was still nourishing from my mother's breast. Whenever I was full and started playing with her breast and took a bite, like most children, I would be chastised on such a level that I would understand I'd done something wrong. The next time I understood that I wasn't supposed to bite the breast that fed me.

'The scripture is research based on human behaviour. It was put together to control the behaviour of the people at that ancient period,' I told my rider.

Everyone can find a chapter in the scripture that they can use as a metaphor for behaviour. Having known my rider for some time, I knew the father of her children had passed away when her children were very young. That brings a different atmosphere to the situation in contrast to those who have separated for personal reasons. The premature death of her children's father was seen as nature taking its course. However, those who have separated often use the resentment of their personal issues to traumatise their children.

In the case of the young teenage soldier, instead of looking forward to going to university, he was sent to prison. It didn't matter how streetwise the teenage soldier was, the police force and the crime prosecution unit did catch up with him. I took the mother of the teenager on a trip one afternoon.

'He is safer in prison than on the street,' she told me.

'What makes the street more dangerous is not just the trading of illegal drugs, but roaming around with lots of money ... money that can't be justified and can't be paid into a bank account. They run the risk of being robbed,' I told the mother.

'I have hope because they will not chop his limbs off in prison ... or kill him. Apart from depriving him of his freedom, he will be safe and will eventually came out,' she told me.

I once took a rider who had just left prison and requested a trip to attend his probation appointment. He gave me a little glimpse of how the prison system operates.

'I want to stay away from trouble. I don't want to go back in,' he told me. 'How long were you in for?' I asked him.

'Nine months, I was given two years ... I'm spending the rest on tag,' he told me.

I learned from him how he wanted to refrain from committing another offence because he would be back in prison if caught.

'Stay away from the street and you'll be fine,' I told him.

He did not want to go back to prison; he needed family support in order to avoid joining the same group who had landed him in trouble.

When the convicted teenager was released from prison, I took his mother for a ride. She was open and happy to tell me her story because she had got her son back, hopefully permanently. I understood her struggle but as long as the drug lords were still operating, her efforts might be in vain. I saw my young self in a similar pathway during my childhood, but in a different environment. When I was nine years old, I lost my father. A life-changing experience when it happened in Africa, unlike in Western Europe where there's a government support system that provides a safety net for those who find themselves in my situation. I struggled emotionally and financially due to my father's absence. I was roaming the street long after school and arriving home late. I was unconsciously looking for someone to fill the gap my father had left in my life. My mother became the sole breadwinner in the family, meaning she was hardly in the house. I roamed around after school, playing football and chilling out with friends. That put me in a vulnerable position to fraudsters and other criminal gangsters. One evening, I came home and found seven crates of empty bottles hidden at our compound. The son of our neighbour, whom I knew very well, and was much older than me, in fact he was eleven years older, asked me to deliver those crates to a well-known public house in the town. For an unknown reason, he gave me directions and the route I should use. I did as I was told. On arriving at the destination, it was as if the bar owner was waiting for me. He took it and I left, end of. A week later, I became wanted by the Gendarmerie National. In Cameroon, a wanted person was presented with a written instruction to attend the gendarmerie, and the document was given to me by the accuser. The accuser was the father of the baddy who commissioned me with the crates. When I explained to the gendarme what had actually happened, the officer spoke back. He asked the father of the perpetrator if he believed my story. The father agreed but insisted that I was the criminal because I took the crates that didn't belong to him. I was very lucky that I was investigated by a responsible and less corrupt officer. He understood that I was used innocently by the perpetrator. The officer gave the accuser a written instruction to bring his son in to be interrogated. The accuser said he didn't know the whereabouts of his son since the incident. It wasn't true, he knew his son would have been locked up and probably taken to prison. Although I was given a small amount of money by the perpetrator of the crime, it was nothing compared to the amount sold. A crate of empty bottles worth about two thousand francs CFA, equivalent to £3. He got £21, but he gave me three hundred and fifty francs, CFA, equivalent to seventy pence. For the sake of seventy pence, I could have found myself in a juvenile institution. At the time, three hundred and fifty francs was a lot of sweets, cakes and many little things any boys my age would've wanted. That was just one of many things that the older baddies were pushing me to do. They knew I was vulnerable because I didn't have a father figure in my life.

The only reason I did not become a criminal myself was because my mother decided to send me to her elder brother in the village. At the time, I was upset because of the different lifestyle in contrast to the city life where I had many choices of activities. However, I achieved highly at school in the village. I had a father, mother, brothers, and sisters to go home to after school. My uncle had eight wives and over sixty children. The school was about two miles away and we went there by foot and sometimes without shoes. With time, I was happier than being in the rural town where I was born. There were three classes and three teachers for the entire school due to the isolated distance of my village but I was very comfortable. After spending two years with my uncle, I was a changed teenager and my life took a different direction; I connected with my ancestors and my cultural roots. I had become a true African, a conscious Nubian. When I went back to the city, I was different to the rest of my childhood friends. They couldn't understand why my view of life was so inspirational. I am who I am today because of that decision my mother took at that pivotal moment of my life. The teenager's mother did not have the same options as my mother due to her migrating status into Britain. She also did not have the financial freedom my Ghana rider had to send her teenager to a private school abroad.

ELEVEN

COUNTER-STEREOTYPE RIDERS

Some of my riders have been so awesome that I'll carry their memories for as long as I'm alive. I've transported all sort of riders from sarcastic, narcissistic, messianic, misogynistic intent, but little did I know the best was yet to come. I like music from Africa and the Caribbean. Driving back to base after dropping off my riders can be boring. At the time I was a smoker, so cigarettes and music were my only companions and I used them to fill the gap. One late morning, I was given a job from Camberwell Road SE5 to South Norwood SE25. My rider was a middle-age white woman who sat in the front seat of my cab and greeted me politely. As I was returning from another job with my African music still on, I thought the choice of music wouldn't be her taste so I changed the music to a radio station. I tuned to Kiss FM as I was certain their play lists were western music. I thought that if she was familiar with the music, it would keep her comfortable during her trip. This was something I did frequently and most people would start humming along. To my great surprise, she reacted differently.

'Why did you change that music? I was enjoying that tune,' she said. 'I was enjoying that beautiful song of Moni Bilé.'

This was a very memorable trip for me because throughout the journey, we had so many things to talk about. After that drive, she started to request my service when I was on duty and she was prepared to wait until I was available. It was such a strange experience for me coming from a sector of society who usually has strong views. Alternatively, I've had completely opposite experiences with other riders. These are the types who shaped my views about making judgements on people before getting to know them; about having a preconceived idea about what character they fit into before actually exchanging a word with them. One day, I took her for her regular trip, and on that day, she offered me a cassette tape. This was the real deal for music; she had made me a compilation of renowned Cameroonian music. It became my favourite cassette during my shift, bringing back memories of Cameroon. Although I had a culture completely different from Wendy, we were developing an invisible relationship that surpassed our cultural differences.

Many riders come to Walworth Road because of the multiple businesses that it accommodates. Whenever Wendy was near our cab office, she would walk there to book her trip. On that particular day, she was moving into her new house, and I helped her with the transportation of DIY materials from the warehouse. We cabbies are highly advised not to step foot into a rider's house, to protect us from possible accusations of malicious behaviour. Wendy's behaviour gave me no cause for concern regarding that warning. With so many heavy goods to be taken into her house, I was happy to offer her a helping hand. In her house, a street sign plate with the word WOMEN caught my eye. I don't know where she got it from but it was very unusual. After driving a taxi in London for several years, I know a transgender woman when I see one but there was nothing about her that I could associate with gender dysphoria, Wendy was definitely not a transgender person. I thought maybe she just wanted to remind her guests of her authority as a woman. All the time I'd known her, she had never been pejorative towards my gender as a male.

'I've never come across any road or street in London called Women ... where did you get this sign from?' I asked her.

She smiled.

'It represents the struggle that women are facing daily all over the world,' she replied.

I know women all over the world suffer similar unwanted abuse from the hands of some sectors of men. I've listened to all sorts of male riders in my cab and some of their conversations about their women friends were painful to absorb. The explicit words they used to describe women was like they were another species. They were comfortable throughout the trip, ignoring my presence. These men may be parents bringing up young boys – it's a scary world we live in. Although they may have been a bit drunk, alcohol only gives them the courage to speak their mind. Wendy's sign stands as solidarity in her fight for women's inequality all over the world and her struggle as a member of a marginalised group gave her empathy to the struggle of others.

I regularly drove a white female rider to her place of work. She was about sixty years old. She was one of the politest riders I've ever driven and her contributions to our conversations were very educational. One day during her trip, I got the opportunity to enquire about something I had been wondering.

'What line of work are you in?' I asked her.

Without hesitation, she replied. 'I'm a barrister.'

That early morning, I was listening to the BBC London breakfast talk show discussing patriotism. There was a contributor who drew our attention with his strong views about migrants. He did not believe ethnic minorities were patriotic enough because they treated Britain as their second country. We quietly listened until the presenter took another contributor who was angry at this suggestion. He said migrants were very patriotic because many of them represent Britain in different disciplines. Both contributors introduced their ethnicity as white to support their arguments. On the countless occasions that I'd driven my rider, I hardly knew her position on this subject matter. She was a person with such balanced views that it was difficult to know whether any subject was challenging to her. However, the callers on that talk show prompted her to open up a little about her experience growing up in her home county of Somerset.

'I grew up with parents who never had any friends or experience with people who looked different to themselves but had many derogatory stories about them,' she said. 'They' (referring to the callers with strong views) 'have to be very strong not to grow up with strong views concerning non-whites. Young people absorb information literally and it's difficult to shake it off as an adult,' she continued.

'How can someone know what another person is thinking? No one lives in another person's body,' I replied.

'I worked hard to pass my A-levels with the grades needed for my first choice of uni. Oxford was close to London, and after graduating, London became my home. I've never looked back,' she said.

'London has its own challenges,' I said.

'Of course, yes. Many taxi drivers from your cab office have made racist comments about black people with the perception that I shared the same views as them,' she replied.

One Sunday morning, the controller gave me a booked trip from her address to King's Cross Station. It was a return trip. In my job, some riders brighten my day when I drive them; I was just happy to drive such a humble human being. On that day, we didn't have time for conversation as we normally did as she was on the phone the whole time. When I arrived at the station, she gave me directions which she received from the person on the phone. My rider got out of my cab and walked towards a black woman and they hugged. They looked very happy and chatty, and then they walked together towards my cab. I got out and helped load her luggage into the boot.

'Andrew, meet my daughter,' she said to me and then presented me as her regular cab driver. As I drove them back to her address, their conversation was like two friends. Her daughter always addressed her as Mother and there was clearly a bond of love between them. I didn't know if she had other children because we were not close enough for me to ask. From that day, I understood why she was such a balanced human, a person with love for humanity. The next time I accepted a trip from her, she was on her own.

'You have a very good relationship with your daughter,' I told her.

I just wanted to initiate a conversation about their relationship, and she didn't shy away from telling me about her.

'I got her at the age of six and I think it was the best decision I've ever made. She filled the gap that was missing in me before I met her. The love is priceless and forever,' she said.

My suspicion that she was her adopted child was true. She had more melanin than average mixed-heritage children.

During quiet periods at the cab office, riders can be in control of who they choose to drive them if they want. It was so slow on this particular day that I stayed in my cab waiting for my turn. A young white woman knocked on my cab window. I recognised her as a frequent rider, and I lowered the glass to speak with her.

'Can you drive me to Kingswood Estate. Cabbie?' she asked me.

'Of course. Please get in,' I replied.

On our way to her destination, she moved from the seat directly behind me to the one on the far left.

'I was going into the cab office to book my cab, but I saw those white drivers inside, I didn't want any of them to drive me. Luckily, I saw you sitting in your cab,' she told me.

'Why don't you want them to drive you?' I asked her.

'They are too racist,' she replied without hesitation.

I was confused. I looked at her through my rear-view mirror, she was white.

'Have you had any bad experiences with them?' I asked.

'They've been racist towards me on two occasions,' she replied.

'Hold on, how can they be racist to you? You're white,' I said.

'The way I dress and the way I talk … and because all my friends are blacks,' she said.

During all the time I had known this woman, she had always dyed her hair a black colour. She could easily be mistaken for mixed race with a very light skin.

'Did any of them actually say anything to you?' I asked her.

'Twice,' she replied. 'On both occasions, I was on a trip with my friend's daughter. Maybe they thought she was mine,' she replied.

'What happened?' I asked her.

'I sat in the back with my friend's daughter. She is only three. At that age, they can't sit still, you know.' I nodded. 'The cab man asked me to carry her so she was not all over the cab, but she wanted to stand and look at the rear windscreen. He asked me twice but I couldn't control her. Cabbie, that's how children that age behave. He said Keep that little monkey off my cab seat. I couldn't believe what I was hearing,' she told me.

'And what did you say to him after he said that?' I asked her.

'I told him I was going to report him to the owner of the cab office. He said Go ahead as if I care,' she told me.

'Did you tell him at any point during the trip that the child belonged to your friend?' I asked her.

'No, I didn't. Why should I? It's none of his business whether the child is mine or not. He has no right to call anyone monkey,' she told me.

'I know that. Racists don't have the ability to control what comes out of their mouth. It is in their DNA,' I told her.

'Even to a child, cabbie. I was so, so angry,' she told me.

I have driven her a couple of times with that child and another time with the mother of the child.

'The reason why he was racist to you is because that child has a dark skin ... they think you're mixed race. That's why he used the overtly racist word to address both of you, I think,' I told her.

'That's no excuse,' she replied.

'I know. It's a regular nastiness I face all the time. Sometimes I stay in my cab just to avoid confrontation,' I told her.

I felt sorry for my rider who was clearly provoked in a case of mistaken identity on the part of a racist driver. I don't condone that it happened to black people but it must have come as a bigger shock to her.

We are very big fans of Lewis Hamilton in our house. One Sunday afternoon, I was watching Formula One with my children and in this particular race, Lewis Hamilton did not prevail, Sebastian Vettel being the winner in his Ferrari. My son, who was very disappointed because his idol didn't win, turned to his little brother.

'I hate Vettel,' he told him.

Although I wasn't happy with the result, I had the capacity to know that in competitive sport, not every result will go our way.

'Why do you hate Vettel?' I asked him.

'Because I like Mercedes,' he replied.

'What if, next season, Vettel signs a contract to drive for

Mercedes? How will you come back from that statement?' I asked him.

He looked at the floor because he had no answer.

'No one has the right to hate people, especially those they've never met,' I told him.

I knew he had got that from the playground, from friends who were supporters of Sebastian Vettel. Developing hatred from sport is a societal illness and social media is an example. I knew he was learning how to hate from his peers in the playground. He was seven years old and at that age, hate is often used as a backstop when losing an argument. No one is born racist, but the environment and inhabitants develop this mundane behaviour and pass it on to fragile young minds. I was lucky to have lived through these kinds of situation and have developed an awareness of how the subconscious mind can absorb misleading information that can lead to hate. Although it wasn't the result I wanted, I knew it was a sporting event that I was watching.

A charity organisation called Kids Company was situated near our cab office. There were so many young people who visited the company frequently, diverse but mostly blacks. I was given a job to pick up a rider from the charity organisation's address. A young man, aged about seventeen, with his trousers down under his buttocks revealing his pants, walked towards me.

'Are you my cab? I'm Sean,' he said.

I looked around and nearly all of them were similarly dressed, including the female. 'Yes,' I replied.

He walked back towards his chums and greeted them with their usual fist bump. He took his shoulder-strapped bag from his friend, walked back and boarded my cab. 'West Hampstead, cabbie. Let's roll,' he said.

My rider dialled a number on his phone and engaged on a call. I said to myself, *I hope the controller knows the type of rider that called for the trip.* I started my cab and drove to his destination.

'Cabbie, can you wait for me? I'm going to Bermondsey after this,' he told me.

He walked away towards an unknown address in a tower building. It was a rhetorical question; he didn't give me time to respond to his request for the additional trip. I was left with no choice but to wait for my rider to return. After an hour, I radioed the controller and explained the situation. He told me to return to the charity office and explain what happened. I was surprised when the receptionist at the charity organisation received my complaint with emotional sympathy. She asked me to invoice the job's itinerary and leave it to her. By the end of that working day, the controller called me into his office and handed me an envelope. The fare from the Kids Company trip was paid in full.

A week later, I was asked to pick up a base rider who had been waiting for a while. It was a busy Saturday, and demand was high. A woman with an imposing figure walked towards me and sat in the front seat. She was a white woman dressed in a mosaic fabric robe, and her hair was wrapped with a different coloured mosaic headscarf. She wore semi fingered-gloves, showing half of her fingers. With a soft voice, she greeted me politely. I was listening to the LBC talk show and the topic was about the dress choices of young people. We listened in silence to many callers who knew much about young people and their criminal activities just by their dress choices. Caller after caller used their individual bad experiences as valid evidence that the young people wearing hooded jackets and trousers under their buttocks were criminals. I arrived at my rider's destination.

'The controller told you my trip was a return fare, didn't he?' she asked me. 'He didn't give me that information but I'm happy to wait,' I replied.

When she came back for her return trip, the debate on the radio about young people's strange choice of dress had escalated to the way they walk. The graphic explanation was directly associated with black teenagers.

'None of these callers have got any experience with the people they are talking about,' she said.

I nodded because I deal with the young people they are stigmatising daily.

'They' (referring to the young people) 'are the products of this very society they are living in. They were not born and bred abroad and migrated here with those attitudes,' she said.

'The dress style that these callers are connecting to robberies that they have experienced does not make sense. Wearing their trousers below the buttocks reduces their movement. Most thieves want to get away from the crime scene as quickly as possible,' I said.

My rider was a calm and compassionate person with the ability to analyse information in her own way.

'I think the callers are more concerned about their hoodies than their trousers,' she told me.

By then I was approaching her final destination, whereupon she paid my fare and left my cab. I was happy to have met a white woman who didn't have a blanket view on this marginalised set of people.

Two weeks later, early in the morning, I was having my breakfast and the television was on. My rider was a guest on the BBC breakfast show. I remembered that I had taken her on a trip recently and was interested to know what the topic of discussion was. She was dressed in similar attire to that which she had worn on the day I drove her. She spoke with the same calm voice I had listened to in my cab and her contributions were from her own lived experiences. She was talking about Kids Company and through her interview, it was clear she was the founder of the charity organisation which provided support for deprived children in the area. During her interview, she spoke about her organisation and the service she was providing for the children. I then understood why she had been interested in the LBC talk show which was exclusively about the sort of children who her company was providing support for. She had a lot of experience with those children and she understood the contempt that some sections of society had for them. She was the founder of Kids Company; she was Camila Batmanghelidjh. Before I took Camila on that trip, I had my own reservations about the young blacks who wear their trousers under their buttocks. My distaste for their style was not in association with criminality but rather stupidity. After my experience with Camila, especially when she said they were not born abroad and migrated here with those attitudes, I reviewed my position. I was born and bred in a different environment and that was not the style my chums and I rolled in. However, many older people who were not used to our ways found our styles ridiculous. She was one of the few riders who challenged my previously held view about the different lifestyles normally witnessed in multicultural cities.

I've heard many arguments that are based on something not witnessed by riders but rather from a tabloid, social media or even a television documentary which generally are opinionated and far from fact. I took a rider who tried to justify populist politicians' ideas. He was convinced that the British culture had changed. Although my rider was referring to Muslims, I knew he also had a problem with my ethnicity as well but would not say it in front of me. The United Kingdom has a culture that is governed by the British law, but also allows other cultures the freedom to practise their traditions as long as they don't infringe basic human rights. When people reach that mindset, it's not because of what they have noticed but rather because of the negative teachings of the populist political leaders amplified by the tabloids. I listened to two similar stories which produced different reactions. A black footballer bought a house for his mother which was something deserving of appreciation. However, the tabloid reporting managed to turn it into a negative story. He dares to reward his mother for sacrificing everything for him to enjoy privilege. Not long after, a young white footballer also bought a house for his mother. On that occasion, the tabloid reported the gesture as an example of a loving child. For those whom these types of reporting are against, we see it as childish but for those who already hold strong views about blacks, it's music to their ears. The negative information about blacks in their subconscious memory bank serves as a default position of hate.

TWELVE

This rider developed a friendship with me the very first time I drove her. Shirley was a different type of human being, charismatic and friendly with a humble personality. I was given a trip in Peckham, where she lived. I waited for twenty-five minutes but she didn't come out so I returned to base. The controller, who happened to be the owner, asked me to go back and wait for my rider. With a lot of hesitation and feeling upset about the wasted time, I returned anyway. Shirley climbed into my cab with a smile and was very polite. She sat in the front seat and used the passenger sunshade mirror to put her makeup on while having a conversation with me. It often happens that when a rider sits in the front seat for the first time, we have a conversation. She looked beautiful in her slim-fit dress with her size zero body. It was winter. The temperature was very low and I had the heater on high but she wound her window down. In my mind, I thought maybe the heating was making her uncomfortable so I switched it off.

'Oh no! Please leave the heater on. I like the mixture of both hot and cold,' she told me.

As I was driving along Clapham High Street, she accidentally reclined her seat too quickly which caused her to roll back, finding herself on the back seat. That scene marked the beginning of our lengthy relationship. While I was worried that she could be hurt, she laughed about it.

'You think I'm mad, don't you?' she asked me.

'Not at all,' I replied.

'I didn't mean to do this in your cab. I'm sorry. What's your name?' she asked me.

'Andrew,' I replied.

On arrival, for a job of eight pounds plus waiting time (which would not even amount to eleven pounds), she gave me twenty pounds. She was very grateful. It was not common to have riders thanking me and being generous.

The next time I accepted a trip at Shirley's address, I waited patiently. I was there for over thirty minutes and eventually stopped counting the time. When she came out, she was with a baby and an oxygen bottle was connected to the baby's nose. Her babysitter helped her to the cab with the baby's belongings. At that time, her babysitter was at the end of her nightshift and had to go home so she was left on her own with the baby and all its needs, to attend her hospital appointment at Guy's Hospital near London Bridge. I decided to drive to the car park and helped her into the hospital. She was very happy because none of her previous cab drivers had ever done that. She didn't know she could request that service from the cab office either. Usually, I'm very impatient because most riders find it difficult to pay waiting time let alone including a car parking fee. Shirley was grateful for my generous action and I was just happy to have helped her. I thought they needed my assistance and my first instinct was to offer that. My initial intention was to help her into the hospital ward and get back to work but I ended up staying with her for four hours. I just kept her company as she saw her baby's doctor, then I took her back home. I did not charge her, I didn't do it for money on that occasion. She took my phone number and was very happy. I had the greatest satisfaction that day knowing that I'd spent over five precious hours on that little girl and her mum. Money can never replace internal satisfaction on certain occasions. However, I underestimated the bond that my gesture had created between us. I didn't notice any sign of her overwhelming gratitude for my generosity, although maybe she did feel this and I didn't see it at all.

Two days later, she called me and requested a ride to a restaurant. I didn't hesitate and was there on time and took her to her rendezvous. She gave me a time to pick her back up to take her home – it was only three hours later. Knowing her situation at home, I tried not to be late for her return journey. I requested that the office controller place a restriction on my jobs. I didn't want a job that would take me out of the way and make me late for the scheduled pick up. When I picked her back up from the restaurant, she presented me to Joe.

'Meet my friend Andrew,' she told Joe. Then she turned to me.

'This is Joe,' she said.

Joe was her date and I was surprised she didn't present me to him as her driver. On our way back, just her and me in the cab, she was very friendly, having had a bit to drink. She introduced herself fully to me and made me feel free to open up too.

'Where're you from, Andrew?' she asked me.

'Camberwell,' I replied. She giggled.

'I mean which country are you from?' she said.

'Just joking. I'm from Cameroon,' I replied.

She laughed and on doing so, I realised she had a great sense of humour.

'Have you heard of a little town called Swansea?' she asked.

'I've sent many letters there and I've also received many from there. I've never been there – but I'm familiar with the town,' I replied.

That's where she was from, the home of drivers' and vehicles' registrations. At the end of that journey, I realised that I'd made my very first white female friend. I felt like I'd known her for many months. When she was leaving my cab, she gave me a sealed envelope. In the envelope there were ten notes of twenty pounds! On average, I'd struggle to earn that amount in two days.

Shirley started using me as her personal driver, taking parcels to her music band colleagues. She had a tribute band of two men and two women and Joe, her date, was part of the band. She had two babysitters who looked after her baby but were employed by the local government service. I was given the task of taking them home at the end of their shift. One was a native African woman and one was a white woman. Shirley organised the personal needs of her daughter and those of her professional career around me. Her personal needs incorporated the medical supplies from her general practitioner to the pharmacy. I was in charge of picking up her babysitters whenever they were running behind schedule. I was also involved in her personal financial dealings. She introduced me to her bank manager, authorising him to hand me any amount of money that they agreed over the phone. I was in possession of her Visa card permanently and her Personal Identification Number to draw cash whenever she was in need. Her professional activities in the band meant she was always on the move and spent many nights away from her daughter and domestic responsibilities. I was, therefore, in charge of driving her costume designer to mend or buy any new costumes for the entire band. I was also on standby twenty hours a day to take the band to or from a gig when they could not drive. Shirley wanted someone she could trust and rely on for her very busy lifestyle and she put that trust in me. A responsibility I'm proud to say I never abused. Although Joe was known as her band member, only I knew he was her boyfriend. The baby's father was involved in the upbringing of their child but their relationship was long over. I knew every piece of information about Shirley's previous lovers up to date because she never hid anything from me. All along, I was still working at the cab office. I would sign in like every driver on my day shift, but as soon as there was a request from Shirley, or any member of the team, I was off. She knew I was cabbing when I was not engaged with her so she was always scheduling her jobs. It allowed me ample time to organise myself, and she told her staff to do the same. Things weren't always glorious in my own life. I was in a relationship at the time and I struggled a lot with the unpredictable job schedule from Shirley. My then girlfriend used to refer to my working partnership with Shirley as "more than just a job".

My relationship with Shirley's mother was not an immediate bond. The first time I met her was at Paddington station.

She had travelled by train from Swansea. Shirley grew up with her parents on the south coast of Wales. It was a long way away if I had to drive to pick her mother up to bring her into London. On that particular day, I was given every information about the description of her mother and stepfather and they were easy to spot! As a cab driver, I've got sharp vision on those types of pick-ups. I approached them and called their names. I was very happy to have finally met the parents of a wonderful woman. I first greeted her stepfather with a warm handshake since he was closest to me. I then approached her mother, still with a big smile and my right hand stretched out for a firm handshake but it seemed she didn't see or acknowledge that I wanted to shake her hand.

'Where's your car?' she asked me.

After about five seconds, I slowly dropped my hand and reached for their luggage. At that point, my natural big smile had turned into a plastic one. However, I directed them towards my cab. During our journey towards their daughter's house, she sat in the front seat, but she only spoke to her husband who occasionally spoke to me. I wasn't worried about their attitude though because I was on one of Shirley's duties.

By her second trip to London she was the one hugging me at a busy Paddington station. I don't know what happened between our first meeting and the second, but it was completely different. There was only one thing that she did not agree with me, she was always reminding me that she was not my mother. I referred to her and called her "ma'am" which she didn't like. I was trying to use the shortened word for madam, but it sounded like "mam" because of my accent, and this means "mother". I have a strong West African accent which, on its own, was a bit difficult for her to fully understand. She had a Welsh accent which I had to pay attention to, to understand what she was saying. Different regional accents played a major role in our conflicting communication on both sides. Whatever she thought of me was irrelevant due to the love Shirley had for me but my internal motivation was always to try to please her, as I did with Shirley and her entire entourage. I was on a mission to fulfil the trust and responsibilities Shirley put in me.

Shirley has never discussed political issues with me. She said it created division amongst friends and families. A gig was organised for her band to play in Cape Town, South Africa. It was the first time Shirley had travelled in the continent and she was looking forward to experiencing the African lifestyle. When I dropped her at the airport, I could see happiness and excitement in a woman I knew had love for mankind. I've never been to South Africa but I knew whatever she was going to experience was never going to be what she anticipated. A friend who had visited Cape Town had told me that it bore no similarities to an African city. When I picked her back up from the airport, I didn't see the happiness she had left with. She looked like the gig had never happened or maybe the airport authorities had refused to allowed them into the country. On our way back to her home, she was just looking forward to seeing her daughter and forgetting about the whole experience.

'How was it?' I asked her.

'As for the gig, it was superb. Cape Town, where we stayed, I didn't like it at all,' she replied.

'Why's that?' I asked.

'Every house had a gate. Visitors must actually give a reason for their visit,' she replied.

'That's how rich people live in Africa,' I said.

'No! It wasn't about wealth. It was a black and white divide,' she replied.

'The only blacks I saw there were the workers,' she continued.

On our way back to her house, I stopped at a Toyota dealer to pick up a car part for my cab. Being the generous person she was, she offered to pay for it.

'What's that part for?' she asked me.

'The front wheel hub unit,' I replied.

'How do you know it's damaged?' she asked me.

I turned off the radio and drove slowly. There was a grinding noise on the front wheel.

'You hear that noise?' I asked her. She nodded. 'It's the bearings making that noise. That's the fault,' I said.

That changed the subject. I knew she wanted to erase what she had experienced. She didn't like the way black people were treated in an African city. I saw humanity in a woman who was born and bred in a country where her only experiences with African people were in the media.

Everything was going smoothly as I bonded with her entourage like a big family, but I was taken aback one day when her African babysitter called to invite me out for a date. She had already planned it, the venue being at a Nigerian restaurant in New Kent Road. After the call, I had many thoughts running through my mind. She was a pretty woman from my perspective, but it came out of the blue. African women are not known for approaching their men for a date. Not that it doesn't happen but it's rare for those born and bred in the continent to have that mentality. Moreover, if she did have a crush on me I should have known because we got on very well during our professional duties. Nonetheless, I didn't want to anticipate her reasons and the date was agreed. It was my very first experience of being approached by a female for a date. I had many thoughts running through my mind, but I grew in confidence on my preparation for the date. I arrived at the venue and to my surprise, she was there waiting for me on a table for two. That was another surprise because African women are not known to be on schedule, especially on dates. I was welcomed with a hug and she had this big smile but to be fair, she always had a big smile. She was looking stunning compared to how she usually looked previously. She was the one that guided the tone and direction of our conversation. She was the dominant partner of the date. I was relaxed because she had organised it and she was also paying for the meal. She was maybe two years older than me but that wasn't a problem. At one point during our conversation, she realised that she was treating me like her junior when she repeatedly asked if I was comfortable and if I was OK. While she was asking me all those questions, I wasn't sure if she wanted a serious relationship with me because I'd never shown any interest on her. If that's what she wanted, how will I approach such a relationship when she seemed to be in full control? After eating our meals, she returned to her questionnaire.

'You're a trusted person,' she said. 'How come you're holding the bank card and managing her finances without temptation?' she asked me.

I adjusted myself on my seat. I was the last member to join Shirley's team and she trusted me quicker than anticipated.

She wasn't someone that was naïve, she was really clued-up. I've never been trusted at such even within my family. Her trust in me was something only she knew why.

'If you were from my country, you would have been a wealthy man by now,' she said.

'I sweat for my money and I have no intention of profiteering,' I replied. Shirley had inherited the house of her late boyfriend's parents which she sold shortly afterwards. Everyone knew this and knew she had a lot of money in the bank. At the time, she had just bought a brand new sports car, I had one key and I was insured to drive it whenever I wanted. I could go to her bank manager and collect up to ten thousand pounds when she needed cash for any purpose. My date was well informed. 'Are you going out with Shirley?' she asked me.

I wasn't surprised at this question because every one of her entourage could think that way. Shirley never hid or shied away from my presence when she was having her bath or dressing up and to make things complicated for her entourage, she greeted me with a hug and a kiss.

'No!' I replied.

I thought she was eliminating the possibility of any intimate relationship with other women before she invited me into her private space.

'Why not? She really likes you,' she said.

'Is that what you invited me here to tell me?' I asked her.

That gave her the opportunity to dive straight into the reason for the date. She wanted me to talk to Shirley about a problem that she had at her workplace. Some people use others' kindness as a weakness. There's a reason why there are red lines in the workplace code. She was working as a babysitter for the local government and was assigned to look after Shirley's daughter. The baby needed attention twenty-four hours a day, all year round. Although Shirley was very generous to her babysitters, she was doing this voluntarily. My date was forbidden, by her employer, to ask for the allocated family money for any reason. She did and that landed her in deep trouble.

'I needed help to bring my daughter over from back home. I was down financially,' she told me.

'And you asked her to give you money?' I asked. Her look confirmed the answer.

'I will attempt to initiate the conversation with her and I'll let you know the outcome,' I said.

As for our romantic meal, my instinct was not wrong; if it seems too good to be true then it's not true. African women do not invite men for a date as easily as that. After the meal, we walked to her house hand in hand and gave each other kisses on the cheek but nothing else. She just wanted to keep my hopes high so that I could clean up her mess. There was no possibility of Shirley changing her statement and ridiculing herself in front of the senior social worker who knew how difficult her situation was. I was unable to help her and our friendship slowly ground to a halt. There was never anything in common between us.

The baby passed away. Shirley buried her in her hometown and held a big funeral send off at the Hilton. I was the only black guest there and after her mother had a bit to drink, she revealed her real self. She was someone who was proud of walking with me at Swansea market and presenting me to her friends. I was probably the only African to have stayed overnight as a guest in her house. I didn't drive to Swansea on that occasion, instead, we, her staff, all attended by train.

I was free to drink a bit of beer but nothing over the top as it was the funeral of a baby I had known. Shirley's mother was talking to some of our friends and then she saw me. Our eyes met, and we started walking towards each other, then I saw Shirley behind her. I believed she wanted to have a chat with her mother. As I approached her mother, she looked at me, not realising her daughter was behind her.

'Where have you been all day?' she asked me.

'I've been chilling,' I replied.

'You've been hiding behind your shadow,' she said.

As I looked beyond her to Shirley behind her, she turned and faced her daughter.

'Mum! This is not the place for that joke. You cannot say such a thing to Andrew,' she told her mother.

Shirley held me by the hand and walked with me towards the counter.

'Mum has had a bit to drink,' she said.

'Don't worry about it,' I told her.

'Have something to drink,' she told me.

She made a gesture to the counter service attendant.

That was the window of true nature – too much alcohol will create a moment where one can release their true self. However, I knew Shirley's mother was a warm-hearted woman because she was very happy and proud to be with me in front of her friends in Swansea. During my stay in her house, I felt her warm human instincts towards me. She did nothing in front of me that I could associate with someone with hatred. Her husband and Shirley's elder brother whom I drove many times around London were respectable gentlemen. During the ceremony, I felt very much part of the family setting, but visibly my presence was very noticeable because of my ethnicity.

THIRTEEN

NIGHTMARE

The troubles I encountered working at night were a stream of problems and for a variety of reasons. However, my best friend was a night worker and found it difficult to work during the day. You may think that he was allergic to sunlight when I explain the problems I encountered at night. The first obstacle I came across was on a Saturday night at around 2 a.m. I picked up two riders from a wine bar in Walworth Road to go to Lewisham SE13. One was a black male age around twenty-five and the other was a white woman roughly the same age. They got into my cab as though they didn't know each other but just wanted to share the cab. The woman sat in the rear seat and the man sat in the front seat. I had a talk radio station on with the volume on an average listening position. After driving for half a mile, the male rider changed the radio station to Choice FM, without asking my permission. I was taken aback by this attitude but I stayed cool – the rider should be comfortable. A few minutes later, he turned the volume up to almost maximum until the speakers started to vibrate. I reduced the volume back to an acceptable level on the steering control. He was not happy;

he turned the volume back up to the loudest position and started to gesticulate to the music.

'I'm using a two-way cab radio to communicate with the controller. The car radio volume must be below or at the same level as the cab radio volume,' I told him.

'You've already got a job. What's the point of the cab radio while you're still on a trip?' he asked me.

'Communication between the controller and I is very important. He needs to know my position at all times. It's helpful for the controller,' I replied.

My rider wasn't even listening to me and he turned the car radio volume right up again. Before his hand returned to his body, I had already turned the volume back to a very low position. He looked at me angrily and attempted to turn the volume back up again, but accidentally switched the radio off. He thought I'd done that from the steering wheel control. He tried to reach the control on my steering wheel. I sensed trouble and quickly pulled over safely. He was very angry.

'Why did you switch the radio off?' he asked me.

I didn't answer because I hadn't switched it off.

'It's not like I'm getting a free ride. I'm paying for this cab, bro. I just want to listen to music, you dickhead,' he shouted at me.

He was very aggressive and he opened the door but did not get out. The female rider got out and waited on the pavement. The black male rider threw a punch towards my head, hitting me on the side of my face. I reacted quickly by moving backwards and avoided the full force of the jab. He got out and joined his female friend on the pavement.

'Come on, big man. I'll knock you down,' he growled at me.

I was angry briefly but managed to control my temper. The female rider, for some unknown reason, did not say a word during the whole scenario. I could not retaliate against someone whose punch did not even hurt me. I switched my cab radio off and headed home. I called it a bad night at the front line. It was a busy period and the controller called me on my phone because I wasn't responding on the radio. I told him what happened which he understood.

On my way home I was reflecting on the whole scenario. These riders come out of nightclubs having spent about four to five hours surrounded by loud music noise and probably dancing. Their adrenaline from the rhythm was high and was fuelled by alcohol. The black male wanted to continue in that mood in a different environment. I refused to drive in that atmosphere which was likely to be a distraction. I always nod to black riders before we exchange words. As Africans, we are in the minority and are supposed to protect each other. When my rider sat next to me at the front seat, separating himself from his female friend, I misjudged his intention. I nodded to him but he failed to acknowledge my gesture. I also tried to make eye contact with him but he avoided looking at me, instead looking across my face. When I'm talking to a difficult black rider, eye contact always helps me form my first impression. The way they react usually gave me an idea of the type of relationship we may have. At the beginning of this incident, no words were spoken; he was just acting and I was reacting to his actions. He didn't speak with his female friend either. Throughout, I was considering how weird that couple's relationship was. There was no communication between them. However, African men are known for occupying the front seat when boarding as a couple. I will not comment on the female silence because I'm not from the school of thought of those who know what people are thinking. However, if she liked the action of her friend then she must have wanted to be accompanied by a bulldog terrier. The best way to understand the reaction of a person when faced with a situation is to see how that person reacts to other people. The African rider who attacked me was not aware enough to know he was attacking an African like him.

I used to regularly drive a white female rider who lived near the cab office to her place of work. I was one of her favourite drivers because our conversations were always constructive. Her children were all mixed race and a bit difficult in character. Most children in that council estate displayed difficult behaviour but her children stood out because of their mixed heritage. Some of my colleagues avoided taking her children because of their behaviour, but I never had a problem with them. Whenever they did not behave or didn't want to pay the fare, I would go straight to their mother with my complaint and she was always happy with my attitude. Her youngest son, who, at the time, was in his early teens, was the one who always got in trouble with the drivers. The first time I drove him, I made eye contact with him for about ten seconds and he looked back at me and gave me the most beautiful smile. He boarded my cab and asked me for my name. Most private-hire drivers are known by a call sign and that teenager knew every driver by their sign.

'What's your name?' he asked me.

'Andrew,' I replied.

'Hello, Uncle Andrew,' he said.

From that day on, he always referred to me as uncle, and he spoke to me with respect. When we were looking at each other, it was to create a bond and for him to see me as family and not an enemy. I learned that from my parents who made eye contact with me to communicate their message due to my being hard of hearing. That connection was lacking from my violent rider who, for some unknown reason, refused to make the eye contact I wanted. He acted as if I was invincible or maybe he was trying to prove to his white female friend how disconnected black people are. I didn't give him what he craved; he wanted a fight to satisfy his desire of being a misinformed African but he was met with a resilient African.

The temptation to venture into the night shift again came after my friend convinced me that the last incident was not a regular occurrence. So, on Friday night at around 11 p.m., I accepted a trip. The rider was in a public house in New Kent Road London SE17. At the time, it was the national closing time for public houses. The law prevented publicans from serving alcoholic drinks to their clients after 11 p.m. Requests for rides became very high from public houses during that period. I picked up my rider, an old man of probably sixty to sixty-five. He was drunk but not so much so to have to cancel the trip. By the way, I did not expect to pick up sober riders from the pub.

'Can we make a quick stop at Ali's 24-hour shop on Walworth please? I will be just five minutes,' he asked me.

The additional stop increased his destination by a mile. When we got there, the shop had a heavy police presence and was not serving any clients. He was not happy and asked me to drive to another shop a mile and a half away.

I told him the fare would be at least fifteen pounds, an increase of seven pounds. He didn't acknowledge nor did he refuse. He was more concerned about getting to the shop. When I arrived, he walked into the shop and all the shop assistants started following him. I sensed that he was probably known for the wrong reason there. He came out of the shop with a bottle of vodka. From a distance I could see that he was exchanging non-friendly finger gestures with the shop assistants. When he got into my cab, I didn't drive as he expected.

'Come on, let's go. Take me home,' he said.

'I need the cab fare before I continue,' I said.

'I haven't got any more money but I will drop it into your cab office tomorrow,' he said.

'No way. My fare now! Please,' I replied.

'Okay, let's go, I'll give you the money when we get home,' he said.

'Huh uh. You should've said that before taking me all over the place,' I replied.

He obviously didn't have money. He got out of my cab and started to walk towards his destination. I was not happy. I followed him and grabbed the bottle of vodka.

'It's for my cab fare,' I told him. He was very angry and he tried to chase me but I ran faster than him. The shop assistants who witnessed the whole show were cheering for me.

'Come back here, you fucking little munchkin. Give me that fucking drink or I'll fucking kill you,' he shouted at me.

I jumped into my cab and drove away. I told the controller what had happened over the radio and he was cool with the way I had dealt with the scenario.

Alcoholic riders are no different from drug addicts. They call for a ride and even though they have got the money for the ride, they will want to satisfy their desire rather than pay for the trip. When the rider is younger, sometimes I make the right judgement by asking for the fare upfront to avoid confrontation at their destination. This older man was well known by the cab office and was on the controller's list of trouble riders, but this time the request had been made by the bar attendant from the public house. This older rider was using a walking stick and he had an earring on one side. He kept a low profile during the trip by keeping his conversation with me to a minimum. When I confiscated his drink, he became very angry, threatening me with violent words and moving faster than his disability should have allowed. Even though he was temperamentally aggressive, he didn't use any racist or derogatory words towards me. He was just swearing after every word. My rider lived in SE11, close to SE17, an area with a high percentage of African residents. Even though the controller was happy with me grabbing my the bottle of vodka to pay for the trip, I honestly did not feel comfortable with my action. Driving a cab in London has turned me into someone unrecognisable. My friend told me once that you don't have to be mad to live in London but if you are, it helps. I found myself taking certain actions because of the behaviour of some unsolicited riders.

My next trip was from the Red Lion, a public house close to our cab office. My rider boarded the cab and sat directly behind me. His phone rang and he started talking to his caller. Midway into the journey, he became angry and started to swear and use racist language. He asked me to go to a different destination. At that point of the trip, the fare would've been ten pounds and where he wanted to go now would amount to another ten pounds. I politely asked him to pay the total fare upfront before I could complete the trip. He did not hesitate and quietly paid me the total amount requested. As I turned my cab around, I noticed he looked disappointed.

He moved to the middle seat where he could be close to me. Through the driving mirror, I see that he was looking at me.

'Don't get me wrong, cabbie … you lot black peoples are very dishonest. You lot are fucking ungrateful,' he told me.

I did not answer him, just carried on driving. He called his contact back and started swearing at her. I then realised he was talking to an African woman through his choice of words.

He told her over the phone, 'Listen you black bitch. I said I was coming over so I am coming, right. … You try that and I'll smash your door in, you black cunt. … Mess me about and I'll fucking show you … hello … hello … ah, the scrubber hung up. Piece of shit … you lot make me sick.'

I couldn't hear what the woman was saying but gathered from their conversation that she was not accepting his request to visit her. Being drunk, he couldn't control his temper, and the phone was cut off. He tried to call her back but her phone was probably switched off. He moved from his sitting position behind me to the seat on the far left where he could see me clearly. He tried to start a conversation with me but I wasn't interested. I focused on my driving.

'I know I shouldn't generalise about you lot because some of you are okay, but my experience with those I know, mate, have got chips on their shoulders,' he told me.

I didn't comment about his provocative generalisation. I was thinking of pulling over and throwing that drunken man out of my cab. However, if anything happened to him on the roadside it could be traced back to my cab office and I would become accountable. Even though he was a drunk, he still needed to be protected, irrespective of the racist and sexist vile language that he was spitting out. Five minutes later, he fell asleep when I was not responding to his racist sarcastic views on my race. He did not even realise when I arrived at his destination, because he was snoring in the back of the cab. I rather pitied the racist foul mouth, realising I had full control of his life. I called his name several times until he answered but avoided touching him. He woke up and, realising that he had reached his destination, he opened the door and walked away without saying a word to me. I thought maybe the little nap half sobered him up a bit and he was getting his marbles back.

The road was partially restricted with cars parked on both sides, I did a three-point turn to head back to base. As I glanced back, I saw money on the back seat and knew straight away it was from him. I could've driven back and given it back to him but I didn't. After all the abuse I received from him, it was enough reason for me to do what I'd never done before. I've never deliberately kept a rider's belongings, but on that occasion, I took the money which was one hundred and twenty pounds. It was the week that the tsunami disaster happened in the Far East and there was a national and international appeal to donate to the survivors. I donated that money to the British charity organisation which was sending over urgent necessities for the survivors. That job was the last job I did that night and I vowed not to work anymore at night, and especially weekends, whatever the case. The drunks were unrecognisable; the same person, when sober, usually presents a different image. My drunken rider was a brown haired, short, slim-built white male. I could not pick a fight with him because I would be locked up pending investigation while the rider would be requiring medical attention. Only drugs or alcohol could've given him the courage to be brave enough to be racist towards an African woman while in my cab. Even if his female friend allowed those racist words to be used on her, he should not have had the courage to use them in my presence. When my rider started saying what he thought about Africans, I concluded that alcohol had given him false courage. Driving in a complex city like London has given me the ability to shrug off narcissism even when I could fight back. I'm very proud to walk away from situations that could get me into serious trouble.

Having two countries that I can call home gives me the opportunity to see things from both sides. I was once on holiday in Cameroon and I was driving with three friends in my car when I hit a very slow-moving traffic jam. There was a big pothole on the lane I was travelling on and that forced me to use the opposite lane. When it was my turn to divert past the trouble spot, none of the oncoming vehicles was willing to exercise patience from their right of way. They, too, were in a serious traffic jam. I was left with no option but to force my way into the oncoming traffic to get out of that situation but the oncoming vehicle did not back off to allow me through. We were stopped on the single narrow lane which was not big enough to accommodate two vehicles. The only way out was for the oncoming vehicle to mount the pavement. However, the pavement was too high and the driver was not willing to risk damaging his car.

Behind me there were files of traffic wanting to capitalise on my unsolicited manoeuvre. The oncoming driver was a white male who, at that moment, was manifesting his frustration with hand gestures. He ran out of patience with my unacceptable driving skills and started throwing verbal abuse at me.

'It seems you guys have no driving regulations here. Even when you don't have the right of way, you just force your way onto me,' he told me.

'Thank you for the lecture. We just need to find a way out of this situation,' I replied.

Most of the cars in both lanes started sounding their horns in frustration at the standstill and the temperature was very high.

'Learn how to drive before getting behind the wheel of a motor vehicle, my friend,' he told me.

Little did he know I was a better driver than he could ever imagine. My friends in the car became angry at him because he was treating me as a local driver who usually has a more inferior driving capacity. I've had a British driving licence since 1996 and I've clocked loads of mileage due to my job. The white driver was way younger than me, he could not have more experience on the road than I did. He could not have known that I was a Londoner because I was a native African driving a car in Cameroon. I could feel tension building from my friends in the car.

'Who do you think you are, you white supremacist? Imperialist. Where did you get the courage to address us in that manner?' one of my friends told the white driver.

I quickly asked him to stop. Luckily, the situation was unblocked by a traffic police officer. On our way, I reminded my friends about their intimidating behaviour towards the white driver. I told them that they may have been protecting me because of their territorial advantage; however, in the United Kingdom, I'd be on the opposite side of this scenario and they would not be there to protect me. They had no knowledge of the background of the white driver but they knew he was a white supremacist and an imperialist which was no different from my drunken rider who spoke from ignorance. That driver was partly right. When I arrived in Britain, I failed my driving test twice before succeeding on the third attempt, not because I didn't know how to drive, you know I drove a taxi in the city for two years. The two times that I failed my test were for the same reason; driving without due care and failing to conform to the rule of mirrors, signal, manoeuvre. Those bad driving habits, I inherited from driving in Cameroon, I told them.

I knew they didn't understand why the white driver was making the statement but I did. The only mistake he made, which many people do, was the generalisation. I see a complete change to the person I was before becoming a resident in London. My reasoning capacity has grown significantly and my culture has shifted to accommodate every culture in the world. My friends, who have never left the shores of their homeland, reacted with a misleading knowledge of Europeans. They still hold the same perception that I also held while in Cameroon that every European is a privileged plutocrat. My position has given me a realistic understanding of the majority of Europeans. The white driver may have planned and saved for many years to have taken his holiday here.

Driving a cab for a living is a very risky and unpredictable business. I had a difficult week when my cab broke down after I'd paid the cab office the weekly rent on Friday. I managed to get the required money to my mechanic to put my cab back in a roadworthy condition. By then, it was already Tuesday. I'd already lost three days and I would have to pay the cab office rent again in two days' time. I had no choice but to venture on a night shift to recover some lost earnings. Everything was good that Tuesday night, with no drunken riders. At around 1 a.m., I accepted a trip from Elephant and Castle to Streatham. It was a good job because the trip was a wait and return. So I was getting double fare plus waiting time. I picked up four African men aged between nineteen and twenty-seven and I knew the rider who had booked the fare. He was a frequent rider at the cab office, and I'd taken him many times prior to that night. I took them to their intended destination at Streatham and waited. Two of the younger riders got out and walked towards an estate. The older riders stayed in the cab chatting to each other. The paying rider was in the cab and that kept me at ease. After waiting for about thirty minutes, the older rider who was sat in the front seat made a phone call.

'What's going on, blood? … Cool, cool.'

After that phone call, I was relaxed and felt sleepy so I took a little nap. I had no worries about getting my fare because I knew the rider. He wasn't a fare dodger at all. From deep in my sleep, I heard a continuous banging on the dashboard. The sound of the back doors opening and closing were very loud as the two younger riders got in.

'Go, go, go, go, go, cabbie, gooooo!' the paying rider shouted in a panicked voice.

I woke up in alarm, I started my cab and drove off like I was driving a racing car. I was burning the front wheels, and I could hear gunshot noises repeatedly at the rear of my cab. I've never driven away that fast and in such a panicked state. I was shaken all the way to Elephant and Castle. The paying rider gave me fifty pounds for the entire journey without asking me how much the fare was. I was relieved when they got out of my cab and walked away. That was the last job I did on that night and the last time I did a night shift whether weekend or weekday.

I did not know what had happened for those young riders to be chased at gunpoint. I've taken the paying rider from his address many times, and although I knew he was dubious, I didn't know he was running such a risky business like the one I'd just witnessed. I knew he was distributing drugs and collecting money from his foot soldiers during the day. However, to deliberately put me in a situation where I could be hurt or even killed was very selfish of him. If any of the riders had been shot by the other gangsters, I would've no doubt been a witness to the crime. That would mean a loss of earnings because of days off work attending the police station for interrogatory interviews. I would've given my recollection of the event and the reason for being a suspected getaway driver. There would be even more loss of earnings to attend court as a witness for many days, including facing criminals in the court and giving information about them. When there are two or more drug gangs confronting each other in a bitter dispute, the scenarios, most of the time, carried a lot of fatalities. I thought I was rough when I was growing up on the street in Cameroon. Comparing that to what I've witnessed driving a taxicab in London makes my teenage madness period looks like a playground. As I was driving my riders back to their final destination after the incident, the two young riders who had been chased by the gunmen were very relaxed. I don't know if they had guns with them but when gunfire is deployed by the opposite gang, it is usually a retaliation. These teenagers should be at university enjoying their studies like their peers but instead they were in drug war battles on the streets of London. When I was their age, I used to look at landscape portraits of young Africans in the West and wish I was in their position. Although I was older than them, I could not say anything to them about the incident. I was scared of them and just wanted to reach their destination.

There was a regular rider who used to request a trip to different destinations and his trips were usually return ones. He was an older rider who most of the drivers knew was a very dangerous criminal and he was likely to carry an illegal gun. Whenever he needed a cab from the office, most drivers would make excuses about taking a break because they were scared to refuse the job in front him. I have never refused the rider because, whatever his activities involved, I was never his target. I knew he would never risk prison for someone whom he did not do business with. I took the rider on a round trip one day and, arriving at the first leg of his destination, he asked me to wait. I didn't hesitate because he does that on most of his trips. It was late evening and it was my last trip. I waited for him for an hour and I became anxious because I wanted to go home. Two hours later, I received a call from the controller asking me to return from the job. My rider did not require a return trip anymore. I saw him two days later. He paid me for the trip, and somehow surprisingly, he paid me for the time I wasted waiting for him. He was always quiet during his journey; it was difficult to know what he was up to. I concluded that he ran into trouble while in his dealings and used an escape route, which also avoided implicating me. All the countless times I've taken him, I have never felt in danger or found myself in a situation like the one with the four younger riders.

FOURTEEN

AFRICA, POLITICS AND POWER

Accepting requests from a family address made me feel more relaxed as I had more idea what the rider would be like. I knew the woman who lived at this particular address; she was a native African from Nigeria. The majority of my African riders were Nigerians. Southwark Council has a high percentage of African residents and Nigerians made up the majority. On Sunday mornings, eighty percent of my riders are Africans because they are likely to be going to church. I waited for this lady at her address for longer than usual, exercising a bit of patience because I knew her. After a while, she opened her door and waved to me, signalling her awareness of my presence. That also reassured me that she was conscious of the waiting time and would be coming out soon. In the cab business, time is money and money is the reason I'm out there ready to drive everyone that needs my service. About twenty-five minutes later, she waved to me again from her balcony and a male rider boarded my cab. As a cab driver, I never know how riders will react to waiting time. Some are conscious about it; others are unaware that some waiting time could be more than the price of the trip. Moreover, I had never taken this rider on a trip, so I didn't know if my rider was financially able to settle the total fare. He was a native African from Nigeria and was about sixty-five to seventy years old. He sat in the front seat, not even acknowledging my presence as a driver who was about to give him a service. He did not greet me nor excuse himself for keeping me waiting for longer than usual. I was already anxious before he got into my cab and adding his arrogant behaviour to this, my animal instincts were engaged. I started my cab, waiting for my rider to confirm his destination. Although when booking the cab, riders usually give their pick-up and destination address, I always seek confirmation in case the controller recorded the information wrongly. For some unexplained reason, some riders may want to change their destination.

'Where are you going, sir?' I asked my rider.

'You don't know where you're going?' he replied.

'You're going to Hampstead … is that right?' I asked him.

He nodded.

'The total fare, including waiting time, will be thirty pounds,' I told him.

'I'm in a rush. Stop wasting my time for the sake of thirty pounds,' he replied.

He looked at me like I was a pile of abandoned garbage. Internally, I was boiling. 'Why are you making that face at me? I have the right to withdraw my service. You can wait for the next cab because I'm not prepared to drive people with attitude,' I told him. He was not happy.

'Do you know who you're talking to?' he asked me in an angry voice.

'Yes, an African with attitude,' I replied.

'Look at you. You don't even have the level of my driver,' he told me.

'Call your driver to drive you around and stop wasting people's time,' I replied.

'Look at this ... I would never share the same car with a nonentity like you back home. My driver is a graduate and very respectful,' he told me.

I was a mile away from the pick-up address and in order to kick him out of my cab I'd either have to take him back to the pick-up address or take him to the cab office. As a cab driver, I obeyed the cab office rules, dropping a rider on the road was a sending home offence.

'So, in that backward country of yours, to become a driver you have to be a university graduate with a driving licence? Wow! I thought human exploitation was over. Oh no! You still have sub-servants don't you?' I replied. 'If anyone, you are the slave in London. You are here to do the job that white people don't want to do,' he told me.

'Yes I am. I prefer to be a slave in your dream country and not in that stone-age country you're from. I'm sure you lot are hiding all your wealth over here and dream of your children attending university here ... thieves,' I replied. 'Look at this fool. You can't even be my children's shoe shiner ... and you have the audacity to mention my children in that stinking mouth of yours,' he told me.

'You and your generation are a disgrace to our beautiful continent. You're nothing but vain,' I replied.

'People like you will disappear under the sun in Abuja,' he said.

'Because you're a member of the Banana Republic, aren't you? You're just a plantation worker of your white masters. One day the tide will turn and you'll find yourself in no man's land,' I told him.

'I'll get my son to deal with you. You idiot,' he said.

I looked at him and smiled.

'There'd better be two of them because I'm ready for a battle. I've done so all my life,' I replied.

My rider's destination was in a very expensive neighbourhood. I dropped him at a house even a high-earning employee living in London could never afford in a million years. Whatever he was doing at his pick-up address, only him and the resident there knew. The regular rider to that address was a single woman. I knew that because I had never noticed any male presence associated with her. Mad wannabe African plutocrats are known to have multiple female partners. Looking at the house where he was staying, I wondered why he didn't use a more luxurious cab than my ordinary one. We have these types of characters all over Africa who cannot hide their mischievous behaviour even when they are out of their den. I believe my rider was a political figure in his homeland of Nigeria. Just by analysing his expression and behaviour I could easily make that link. African states are factories for billionaire politicians. As soon as an ordinary citizen gains a political appointment, they usually celebrate by throwing a big family party, knowing that wealth awaits them. Africa, in general, is the most blessed continent on this planet, rich in everything mankind needs to have the best quality of life. I grew up in a clement temperature, very natural, so that I needed neither warming up nor cooling down at any time throughout the year. My father was a farmer in the rural town of Mutengene. I enjoyed all the organic fruits and foods that the rich soil produced. My town was situated between the highest mountain in central Africa and the Atlantic Ocean. The mountain had an altitude of four thousand one hundred metres with the very fertile soil. The ocean has, for hundreds of years, served as the passage for transatlantic slavery and now holds the biggest oil reserve. Without opportunity, as a young ambitious man who strived for a better life, I was left with no choice but to migrate in order to achieve my goal. My parents did not educate me about my history so I could understand the reason for the deprivation of my area. While growing up, I became a fan of Fela Anikulapo Kuti, a Nigerian revolutionary singer. A strong and brave African who hated injustice and was not afraid to call out the political thieves. He was regularly sent to prison for singing about corruption and injustice within Nigerian political leadership. He used his platform to speak out for children like me whose future had been swept away by the ineptitude of these selfish leaders.

The reason I was certain that my rider was a politician was because businesspeople from Africa do not have his attitude. Successful self-made African businesspeople struggle and the difficulty gives them a better understanding of working for oneself. My rider thought he was a different African, a privileged African perhaps, who was financially secure. However, what he failed to understand was that capitalism is a shifting ideology driven by greed. Through my job, I've taken many riders to Eton College and their attitudes were somehow different to students from other colleges. They are brought up differently with no human feelings and educated differently from the rest of us. They believe they are beyond the human struggle. I drove a young man on a trip from Putney SW15 to Eton College once. When

I arrived at the pick-up location, he came out with two suitcases and left them near my cab. He didn't say a word to me and went back into his house. I only guessed he was my rider. I then loaded the luggage into the boot of my cab. After about three minutes, he came out of his house and sat in the back seat. He started searching his shoulder bag as if he had forgotten something. Although I had the postcode of his destination, I wasn't sure of the exact location.

'Hello!' I said. He looked at me. 'Where are you going?' I asked.

'You should have the address on your thing,' he replied.

He was referring to the booking message on my phone.

'I only have the postcode. I need the full address please,' I said.

'Eton College,' he replied.

During the one and a half hour journey, I was the only one talking and he only gave a brief answer to my questions. Yes or no was the only language he seemed to know. He was not on the phone either but rather looking lost on his way to the best educational institution money can ever buy. I felt like I was driving an alien on that trip. When I arrived at his destination, he was very friendly and chatty with his friends, a completely different person from the one I had just spent an hour and a half with. In contrast, students at ordinary colleges usually have a more constructive conversation with me. They never feel superiorly intelligent in front of me as a cab driver. I picked up a student once from Heathrow airport to take her to Oxford University. It was her first time travelling alone to her new institution. She was not shy and continuously bombarded me with questions about things she didn't know. She was very polite and very happy to be going to one of the best universities in the world.

'How are you, Andrew?' she asked me.

I was surprised when she addressed me by my first name. I guessed she had read my name on the private-hire badge which was hung round my neck.

'I'm fine, thank you,' I replied.

'Where are you from?' she asked me.

From my accent, she knew I was not from Britain.

I told her Cameroon.

'How long have you been here?' she asked me.

I didn't find her questions intrusive because she also had an accent.

'Very long … over twenty years,' I told her.

'Wow! That's more than my age. This is my first year here. Everything seems strange,' she said.

'Don't worry, you'll get used to it,' I told her.

When I dropped her, I wished her a pleasant stay and hoped she succeeded in her future discipline. When I was a student back in Cameroon, at the time there were just government and religious schools. Politicians had no choice but to send their children to the same institution as I attended. They used to come to school in a chauffeur-driven car and their drivers treated them like princes and princesses. In the school premises, they hardly played with us. That was my introduction to the class divides and these people continued all along with their class segregation in society. My rider was definitely not a historian. History has taught us that all the politicians who robbed the continent of their wealth did not end up as the African heroes but rather villains.

I once drove a female rider from the West African state of Gambia whose attitude was the complete opposite to my arrogant rider. I was asked to take her on a trip by her family member who also used my service regularly. I didn't know about her professional career back home but she had a pleasant attitude, just like most riders I've driven. After driving her around for a day, she asked me to take her to the airport the following morning. I did not hesitate because of her respectful and gracious attitude towards me. The next day I took her to the airport, helped her at the check-in counter and she was all set to go. She paid the fare, including the parking fee. She thanked me and was grateful for my service. My attitude towards her gave her the confidence to trust me not just to become her regular driver but also for her daughters who both studied at university in Britain. Her children both had down-to-earth attitudes and showed me the same respect that their mother did. All the time I was taking this lady on numerous trips, I thought she was a businesswoman in her home town. I regularly took her on trips with her consignment to the shipper. One morning, I dropped her at a central London office. She told me that I should pick her back up but she would let me know an hour before she finished. Three hours later, I received her call requesting a scheduled pick-up booking from her. While I was waiting for her, three men in suits brought her trolley suitcase into my cab and waited with me. Shortly afterwards, she came out with three other men. They were all from the same West African country because they spoke the same traditional language. They all lived in the African state, and they seemed to conclude their meeting outside. The three men were looking at my cab curiously. When my rider got in, one told me to drive carefully and take great care of madam. She looked exhausted as I drove her to her multiple destinations.

'I had a difficult meeting today, Andrew,' she told me.

'How's that?' I asked her.

'Gambia has just discovered oil ... but the price of an oil barrel is so low at the moment that the cost of rigging the thing is nearly equivalent to the market price,' she told me.

'Wow! That's good and bad news at the same time,' I said.

'All the delegations you saw there are here for the negotiation with the engineers ... but it has been difficult to decide,' she told me.

That was the first time she'd had a conversation with me that was nothing to do with family and business matters. She only shared the information that she had shared with her delegation in that meeting. She didn't tell me about her position amongst the delegated who were negotiating for a contract with the rigging company. I then understood why the men around her were looking at me and my ordinary cab. They were using Addison Lee cab service for their trips which was in the high echelon. After that window of information, she was back to her usual ways. I understood she didn't want me to view her any differently from before. When I dropped her at her final destination that day, I looked at my cab and thought to myself, wow! This woman really is one of the simplest Africans I've come across. I took my rider who introduced me to her on a trip afterwards.

'Who is your sister in law?' I asked him.

'What made you ask that?' he asked me.

'I took her to Victoria last time. When I picked her back up, she was with some official delegation from The Gambia. Then she told me she'd just chaired a meeting with them. What position does she hold?' I asked him.

He giggled.

'She is a minister in Gambia,' he replied.

'Wow! I didn't know that,' I said.

'She doesn't like to make a fuss about it. That's how she is,' he replied.

No fuss – just like the way my rider's contribution to the subject was conducted, which was simple. I understood her ministerial position should not become an obstacle in the future. Although my two riders were political figures in their respective countries, their attitudes were completely different. I saw something different from the female politician. I was requested to take her on a trip to her daughter's university. Her daughter had a lot of luggage. She was moving into her university accommodation at the beginning of the academic term. It was the first time they were going to live separately. It was also worse because they were going to live in a different country. On our journey back to her London residence, she cried all the way. I could not have a conversation with her because I understood what she was going through. Most politicians are so heartless because of the decisions they make that affect many people negatively. They look emotionless in every situation even when dealing with their own family. My rider was different not just in her simplicity but also her humbleness to the most important things in life.

I had a regular rider from the Gambia who was a politician before switching to an international organisation. He was one of the most generous riders I've ever had, and one of the simplest Africans. Most riders whom I've taken were well behaved but few of them leave a lasting memory with their unique natural human charm. When I knew him, he was working for the United Nations before switching to the World Bank. Although his office was in America, he regularly travelled for his work obligations in Asia and the Middle East. I noticed the pre-emptive nature of mankind when we went through the first-class check-in area. With other travellers in front and behind us, we were regularly approached by the airport staff.

'Can I help you, sir?' the airport waiter asked.

'No need. I'm checking in,' my rider replied.

'Are you travelling on business?' he asked.

At Heathrow terminal five, British Airways, the business and first-class passengers share the same check-in area.

'No, I'm travelling first class,' my rider replied.

Walking behind him, I could see the reaction of the waiter. Classism was so embedded in her subconscious that she physically could tell a passenger who can travel first class. Two native Africans walking into the first-class lounge, with me dressed typically as cab drivers do, could not afford to fly in the prestigious part of the plane. My rider was one of the most intelligent Africans I've known but his simple appearance did not demonstrate that. Although my rider did not seem worried about it, the discrimination did not resonate with me. My rider did not just grow in pre-eminence into his position, he had a scholarship from his home country to study in Britain. He subsequently progressed to a commanding position in his professional career. Unlike my foul-mouthed Nigerian politician who thought I was a slave for driving a taxicab on the streets of London, my Gambian rider understood the real struggle Africans faced globally. Africans who are in a position of power and do not understand the struggle of fellow Africans probably gained power in a vacuum. Many African politicians capitalised on their populist ideology. The naïveness of their constituency are fooled by their unrealistic rhetoric. My arrogant rider who thought I was less than a human being was probably parachuted into pre-eminence by such a constituency. His lack of emphasis to those less privileged than himself was evident. I benefited from my Gambian rider's generosity, and more importantly from the quality of our conversation. He explained how money lent to developing countries by the World Bank fuelled corruption. The liquid currency offered, instead of investing through credited companies, was problematic. 'Fact is stranger than fiction where money is concerned'. Wherever there's money, there's corruption, mostly in countries with a poor history of freedom of press and speech and with a questionable human rights record.

When my rider told me that I was a slave because of my taxicab activities on the streets of London, it was an understatement. I was born in a bondage that was passed down through generations in my family. Until we manage to change the despotic system that allows self-appointed governments to make selfish decisions about the future of our continent, children like me will still be in the same predicament for generations to come. My rider may be financially free but forever a subconscious prisoner, because the International Court of Justice in The Hague is more or less the intercontinental African court of justice. I'm like the character, Kunta Kinte, in the film *Roots* who was forced out of his beautiful and pre-eminent village in Africa. He was subsequently taken to America and forced into slavery. In my situation, I deliberately travelled to London because of the situation caused by European plutocrats to do jobs that, according to my rider, were akin to slavery. My rider, however, was, in my opinion, the house slave, a member of the thieves who collaborated with slave traders to facilitate the captivity of innocent Africans from their villages. The International Monetary Fund has provided a platform for Africans power hungry to borrow money in the name of the country for their development but, in hindsight, it is to buy luxury for themselves. When we arrived at my rider's destination, there was a man on the forecourt of his big house. He was near a luxury car with the doors wide open and music was pouring out of the car's expensive loudspeakers. I could only guess that he was the son of my rider who he promised me he was going to deal with me when we got to his destination. He may have a powerful car and live a life of luxury through unaccounted wealth but that could never buy him physical strength. He would need three people like him to put me down. However, when politicians like my rider make such a threat, like he did to me, in any country in the continent of Africa, be very afraid because they will act on it. I may exercise my human rights protection over here but in the African state, I could never vouch for my safety when these power-mad nonentities make such threats.

FIFTEEN

THE MENTAL PREPARATION

Physical exercise has been a vital part of my life, not just for my driving career, but also for my mental stability. Way back when I was four years old, I started playing football with my friends on the street. I continued the habit until puberty when I became aware that I could turn my hobby into a professional career. I abandoned that path after I realised I wasn't gifted enough to compete with the best. The driving career that I embarked on meant I spent most of my working hours sitting down. There was a regular rider whom I used to drive to Brixton Recreation Centre for work. He was a personal trainer. During one of his trips we were having a conversation about his profession. He was built like an ex-military man, strong muscle but very humble.

'Apart from your full time job here, do you have private clients?' I asked him. 'Why do you ask? Do you know someone who is looking for a personal trainer?' he asked.

'I want to have a body similar to yours,' I replied. He smiled.

'You do not need a personal trainer to shape up. Just register with your local gym,' he told me.

'I go to the gym three times a week,' I replied.

'You have to change your exercise regime. As a full time driver, you should use the treadmill regularly,' he told me.

'What about weightlifting?' I asked.

'Go very light on the weight. You want to be mentally strong. That's the way to go,' he said.

The advice acquired during that trip was more important than the fare I got from the rider. Even though I had played football from my youth and felt very fit, that information was a wake-up call for my exercise routine. A retired taxi driver who usually visited our office referred to the trade as brain damage because of the body imbalance. All I had been concerned about was how much money I made. Although I used to attend the gym three times a week, it was to lift weights and build muscle to feel good about myself rather than to exercise my entire body. From that day, I changed my exercise regime and started running three times a week. My resistance training helped me mentally and physically and I've never looked back to my old self.

I was getting to that age where in my cultural setting, I should be starting a family and have my own offspring. My extended family back home was aware of my girlfriend before I travelled and the elders in the family kept the relationship active. Living far from her, I was trying to disassociate myself from that relationship and hope that, with time, it would end. I didn't want to waste her time because she was also at the age where she could find someone else and build a new relationship. However, every time I was in contact with my elders back home, they always reminded me of the relationship with my girlfriend. She was attending every ceremony for my family and regularly visited them. On one of my holidays in Cameroon, I got my girlfriend pregnant and our relationship escalated to a different level when she had our first daughter. I was so happy to have become a father for the first time that I started thinking of bringing them over here. During that period, I was doing eight shifts a week. I was doing my normal shift from Monday to Saturday. On Sundays I did two shifts, starting at a nightclub from 1 a.m. till 6 a.m., and then continued at the cab office until 6 p.m. All this to raise enough funds to bring my daughter and her mother over here to give them a chance for a better life. I was also aware of the obstacles involved in bringing a woman from Africa and living together as husband and wife. One of my colleagues who brought his wife over from Africa was being investigated at that time by the police. His wife accused him of raping her right from when they were back home and continuing the ordeal when she came to the United Kingdom. It was very strange to me because in Cameroon, I'd never heard of a husband raping his wife but now I lived in a country that respects human rights. The allegation was dismissed, I assumed that the man was innocent and would be allowed to continue trading as a cab driver. However, another driver, who was closer to him than I was, told me the wife said she wanted the guy out of her side and out of the family house. Just the defamation of character could haunt this innocent man, forever even though the case was thrown out. As a cab driver, if he was found guilty, it would have been the end of his driving career.

There was another colleague who caught his wife with his friend, having an affair in their marital home. His night shift was interrupted because his cab developed a mechanical fault so he decided to return home. In the taxicab trade, we're very productive during social periods, more so during weekend night shifts. Being unable to enjoy a weekend with family became the number one factor of relationship breakdowns. Knowing all the risks involved did not stop me from thinking I could be the next victim. My daughter's well-being and future were the primary reasons for taking the risk. There were so many things I could have done before making this decision, but I went with my personal preliminary gut reaction. Mr Awah Atanga, whom I failed to consult before making any rational decisions, was and is still not just a friend but an elder brother. We worked together in the taxi trade for a very long time and he was my mainstay, being pivotal to many aspects of my life. He also had experience that was advantageous to me. He was an international trader who dealt with shipping goods from Great Britain to Cameroon. That gave him the opportunity to be exposed to different cultural behaviour, both here and in Cameroon. I hastened the process of my marriage without telling Mr Awah and obtaining a spouse visa was my ever-regrettable mistake. Mr Awah was in an identical position to me and had been in that position since I arrived in the United Kingdom. He had long-term plans for his family back in Cameroon and I could have benefited from his experience. The strangest thing was that he made me aware of the reasons for his long-term plan. He analysed the behaviour of African children being brought up in Britain; whether or not they are born here made little difference. He concluded that they became alienated from their own culture, making them susceptible to unwittingly derail. He said that spouses were like rabbits caught in the headlight – they go from darkness to full bright light. Those spouses who are still contemplating whether they have made the right choice of partner or not can hasten a decision they may regret later because of the opportunity to live in Europe. The deprivation of opportunity in sub-Saharan Africa is a major factor in people wanting to move to Europe. When an intimate relationship proposal comes from a European resident, it is likely to be accepted by the African resident partner. However, when an identical proposal comes from an African resident from the same country, the decisive partner will not hasten their decision.

I'm an individual with a different mindset and I didn't want to stay in the shade of Mr Awah's shadow. I didn't have the patience he had. I hid my decision from him at the time as I've always been a rebel, a risk taker perhaps. My way of doing things was different from Mr Awah's because of my own life experience. The premature death of my father robbed me of the opportunity and protection he had enjoyed from his father. When I announced the news that my then wife was joining me in Britain, many friends and family back home were adamant it was the work of the witchcraft guru, a position I clearly distanced myself from. All those who are from that school of thought practise it as well. Many people in Cameroon relied on the spirituality of the witchcraft doctors. The unanswered questions of the practice cast a big cloud on the reality and that stopped me from believing. In fact, the living conditions of people in my town and country worsen year in year out, even though they spend their time waiting for the miracle promised to come to fruition. The ancient system could not be modernised and it was time I tried something completely different. However, I told Mr Awah of my decision after I'd taken all the necessary legal procedures to bring my family over. I put him in a position whereby he was powerless to have any input. He didn't approve nor disapprove of my decision vocally but his body language was not positive at the rush to bring my family over.

Three years was all it took in the United Kingdom for the relationship to crack. Getting married in Africa is not an easy process. First I had to settle demands from her family which was more expensive than the reception. With the blessings of the family, which normally happened after the full satisfaction of their demands, I was then cleared to proceed with the different stages that an ordinary wedding has. After all those stages, I had to satisfy the visa officer that the marriage was genuine and prove that I could support my spouse without her needing any public funds. When I noticed a shift in her character, I first thought she may have postnatal depression and also may be missing her mother from whom she had never been separated until I brought her to Britain. Postnatal depression first came to mind because she gave birth to two children in less than three years of arriving here. I quickly researched how postnatal depression manifests from a regular rider who was a midwife. However, when I told her about the changes in my wife, she quickly dismissed that possibility. By then, my wife had travelled to Cameroon twice in the three years that she had lived in London. I asked her if she wanted to go on holiday to Cameroon. She said she wanted her mother here to help her with the children. So, I then began the process to bring her mother over here with the aim of easing up the noticeable crack in our relationship. I did all that because whenever a relationship is under pressure, the children suffer. In doing so, this time I consulted Mr Awah, but I told him a convincing story which he found difficult to persuade against. I told him that by bringing my mother in law over here, she would also help babysit the children. That would enable us to give our relationship more attention and the quality time needed to repair the visible crack. It would also save me multiple airline fares to take the entire family to Cameroon. Mr Awah knew I was fighting a losing battle but went along with the idea. He told me there was no harm in trying and he was prepared to help me with any difficulties I had with the application form. At the first attempt, my mother in law failed to convince the visa officer of her reason for returning to Cameroon after her stay. As I'm always a fighter, I appealed the decision in the immigration court and secured an entry clearance for her to visit us. The behaviour of my wife did not change and she didn't show any emotion when I told her of the immigration court's decision. I was surprised but not alarmed because until her mother was physically here, she couldn't be relieved from certain chores. As we were waiting at Heathrow Airport for my mother in law to arrive, my wife's phone rang. It was an immigration officer asking questions. When my mother in law came out and met us, I noticed a change in her behaviour straight away. I asked if immigration had wanted to speak to me. She told me that it would be strange if, when her daughter lived here, she had to provide her husband's phone number. It then made sense to me why my wife was speaking to the immigration officer rather than me, the sponsor who represented her at the court. During her stay until the day she returned, I noticed the strangest behaviour from my wife and her mother, different from anything I'd seen before. l prepared myself for any eventuality that might come my way.

The story of my colleague who was accused of rape by his wife had taught me a lesson. I decided to prevent that from happening to me, and so I deprived myself of what couples enjoy daily. Our marriage wasn't consummated any more. I was later accused for being in a cult that magically supplied me with money in exchange for human life. I wasn't surprised, such accusations can only come from a witch doctor. My wife was spreading these rumours to family and friends back home. If she'd done that over here, people would have thought she needed mental help. Shortly before that period, I was reading a book titled *Secrets of the Millionaire's Mind* by T. Harv Eker; it was one of my favourite reads. I was introduced to the book by Richard Blackwood on one of his Saturday talk shows on Choice FM. He recommended it for aspiring listeners. Richard Blackwood is an African comedian who rose to fame very young and his style appealed to many people. He also declared bankruptcy early on in his career due to mismanagement of his wealth. However, he was very determined to learn from his mistakes and rebuild his life back. On doing so, he was sharing his experience with his listeners and the book was key to his philosophy. In the book, there is a chapter where the reader is asked by the author to make a promise that in five years they will be a millionaire. I asked my wife to help me be the person I was making the promise to but little did I know that she was taking it literally. I was just promising that I would have a millionaire's mind, not physically become a millionaire. She thought it was a book of a cult as revealed in her email to my best friend in Cameroon. Afterwards, social services called accusing me of depriving my children of food. I was not a gambler, an alcoholic nor a smoker; I could not deprive my family of the basic necessities. After the police visited and reported back to the social service worker, they decided to close the case. She came to that conclusion because the police report was the opposite of what I was being accused of. In my exchange with the social worker, she told me the reason for her complaints, but the police found enough food in my house to feed five households. That marked the end of the road for the social services route to force me out of the house. However, I was still optimistic about our marriage because every relationship does experience difficulties sometimes.

On the second occasion, she called the police directly and accused me of hitting her. I was arrested and jailed for seven hours. After investigating the accusation, the police detective concluded that there was nothing remotely true about it and I was released without charge. However, he advised me to move out of the family house if I didn't want to be continuously arrested. I'd never been arrested in my life let alone been locked up in a police cell. It was my first experience. I went through what I usually watched in a crime how when the bad guys are taken to jail. The police took a swab from my mouth and registered me in their database. They took my fingerprints, and then put me against the wall and took my photograph. The whole scenario seemed like a dream to me; I couldn't believe how quietly the scene was developing. In the past I've done so many things that deserved me spending time in jail temporarily. I could've never imagined that I would be sitting in jail because of the woman I brought into the UK. British police stations are not places with the best history for black people. Many Africans have lost their lives while in police custody. If the arresting officer had had the bias of being a victim of domestic violence herself, it could have been a different outcome. In that police jail where I passed the slowest seven hours of my life, I'd hope to come out of there as healthy as I went in. After the police detective in charge of my case concluded that there was nothing true about my wife's allegation, he had only one dilemma about letting me go. The police had been to my address twice on false accusations as it's their duty to attend and assist any citizen showing signs of being in danger. He asked me if I had a responsible adult friend or family member who could accommodate me until I could remove my belongings from my house. I didn't want to live in the family house anymore but the detective anticipated my decision. Mr Awah was the only person I had in mind and he was there to clean up my mess. He accepted the conditional request of the detective to keep me until I moved out of my house.

After that relationship ended, there was no slowing down of my adventure. I was born a fighter and I live by that. My job as a cab driver had helped me overcome the situation. Thanks to my rider who was a personal trainer, as he taught me a lifetime lesson. The marital issues of my colleague who was accused of rape was a bigger lesson than I had thought, even though at the time I didn't think it could happen to me. I didn't anticipate my relationship would hit the rocks that soon, let alone believe that I could be jailed at the point of separation. My friendship with Mr Awah was second to none, a lesson from someone with wisdom. My greatest achievement in life was when I made the decision to travel to Britain. It was not just to escape the deprivation of opportunity, but to prevent my offspring from reliving my own experience. Having my three children living legally in

Britain was all I wanted; their mother was part of the family. Our relationship didn't work out as planned and therefore we moved on in different directions. Our marriage was not arranged and nobody was to blame from my perspective. Even though there were external pressures, it was up to us to know what our responsibilities and priorities were. My ex-wife was not my private property; we only needed the interdependences of each other as companions. The children were a blessing to our union which came with responsibilities. When she consciously decided that my contributions to the upbringing of the children were no more needed, that's when things went wrong. The British government can provide financial help but are in no way capable of replacing me as a father. We migrated from a country where the social service system is only a name on the government portfolio to our adoptive country which provides for those who find themselves in circumstances that are out of their control. She was short sighted, seeing just the short-term financial benefits but ignoring the long-term damage. There's a saying which says, remove the father out of the family setting and see the effects on the boy. I'm a man with so many experiences because I've been through many situations at different stages of my life. I understand my boy child better than my ex-wife and I'm better equipped to educate him. Although I wasn't brought up in a complex city like London, I know the anxieties of a boy at pre- and post-puberty ages. A child's peers can influence their character and could lead them down the wrong path. When my boy was born, I anticipated the challenge I'd have bringing him up in this technologically developing society. Bullying and grooming which can be detrimental have moved on-line. I only had one theory that I was going to use all the way in every stage of his life and that was to remind him of the physical and mental strength that he inherited from me. It can be used to create a pleasant environment for people around him regardless of their gender, sexual orientation, race or religious beliefs. He would walk into the outer world where there will be some people who will want to change that physical and mental strength into a negative force. They will mischievously turn him into a monster that even I will not recognise. It doesn't mean that my girl children will not suffer if my relationship breaks down. As a man, even my twenty-five years' experience of driving a taxicab on the streets of London with the majority of my riders being women, did not equip me with understanding the anxiety women live with daily. With my girls staying with their mother, they will benefit greatly. My ex-wife has lived the experience of being born and bred in a country with less protection for women. She now lives in a country with laws that protect women's rights to be equal. However, the historical predatory nature of the alpha male relationship to the female has kept women on their guard, regardless of their geographical location. Back in Cameroon, I spent two precious years with my uncle during my pre-puberty age. I formed my relationship with my spouse from what I learned from him. My uncle always said: when love ends, you find a new one. I did not carry any resentment from the experience of my previous relationship. I accepted my new norm of being deprived of contact with my three children by my ex-wife. The only thing that would've broken me was to have the stigma of criminality attached to my name. I didn't want to find myself in a situation where the police would have to be called every time because I wanted to see my children. I also did not want to have contact with my children through the judiciary system. I did not have the time or money to fight just to see the children that I worked hard to put in this privileged position.

I later received a letter from a law firm accusing me of harassing my ex-wife for money after I brought her into this country. I didn't understand where that allegation was born from; since our separation I'd not been in the family property. There was an incident which happened in the area where my former house was; she lived inside my cab office pick-up zone. I was on a job with two riders in my cab when I saw my ex-wife walking along with my three children. Until that moment, I had not seen my children for months. I stopped to greet them but she pulled them away from my view. My two female African riders were wondering what was going on.

'Do you know them?' one of my riders asked me.

'Yes! The children are mine. She's my ex-wife,' I replied.

There was a moment of disbelieving silence.

'Don't worry, brother. It's the madness this country has given to African women,' one of my riders told me.

I felt disenchanted about the whole situation but reluctant to approach the judicial authority for help, and ever since I've remained in a state of denial that I could find myself in this position. I was elevated to who I am today due to the help of women, both in my family and friends along the way. For that reason, a woman cannot hurt me or my feelings because I owe a great deal of gratitude to every woman. I wasted no time falling in love again with a pretty young woman in my hometown in Cameroon while on a business trip. Every one of us is unique in their character. I start every day with a clean sheet and a fresh mind and confront the world with a new inspiration, and I always look ahead, on the bright side. As I'm writing this book today, I've got four children with my lovely wife, and we all live in London. I'm not looking for a perfect match in my relationship because it doesn't exist. Every one of us has a different background, back story and their own personal goal. I do not have the same goal as my wife because our extended families are different in behaviour and in their family setting. However, she and I are managing our differences in a way that does not compromise our nuclear family, which is our priority. I learned an important lesson when I lost my father at an early age. None of my father's extended family, whom my father helped, were there for me when he died. I was not their priority; instead, they stayed as far away from me as they could. I didn't expect anything different from them. My past has always influenced my decision and whatever the outcome, I've never had any regrets.

SIXTEEN

DEVELOPING THROUGH AN OPEN MIND

The initial process of writing this book was not based on superstitions, hopes or supernatural power. It is my lived experience which I have acquired during my twenty-five years of driving all types of people from every walk of life. Throughout my career, I've had a personal relationship with every race, profession, sex, gender and disability. I've transported riders from their pick-up point to their destination inside the M25 Greater London and beyond. Taxi driving is often classed amongst the lowest of professions, and the men and women in this trade are regarded as illiterate. Some riders regard us as people with a very low intelligence quotient. My job is mainly driving and the good thing about me is that I can drive all day without becoming bored of it. I'm a very good driver, and that's why riders trust me to take them to and from their destinations. When riders request a cab, often they are late for their appointment, their place of work, hospital appointment, airport and so on. The last thing they want is to get a slow, inexperienced driver. Most often, in a polite manner, riders asked me to reach their destinations quickly and use the best route. I'm a very fast driver on the city's roads and on the motorway. I'm not proud of it but at times I do go above the speed limit. I do this to get my riders to their destination on time but most of them still think I've got a low intelligence quotient. Every time I board a flight to and from Cameroon, if for one minute I thought the pilot had a low intelligence quotient, I would be laughed at because it would sound like an April fool. I've safely driven many riders to and from Stansted Airport who unconsciously undermined my profession. Pilots and taxi drivers are in the same profession in many respects. They are responsible for their passenger's safety. Their job is to transport passengers from their pick-up point to their destination for commercial purpose. Pilots use a navigation system as a guide and are trained and licensed to do their job. Most cab drivers never had the privileged opportunity to train as a pilot and, believe me, a lot of them, if given that chance, would succeed. The Knowledge test to acquire a green badge to become an all-London taxi driver is one of the most difficult tests in the world. Most pilots would find it difficult to complete this because it's a memory test and the examiners are veteran cab drivers who know the streets like the back of their hands. Airplanes can fly themselves and the route of their destination is directed by satellite navigation which the pilot has to follow. For the majority of journeys, taxi drivers don't need the satellite navigation system to negotiate the streets of London to get to the rider's destination; they know it.

My chosen career, unfortunately to some members of my family and friends, was not high standard enough to regard me as an affluent member of society. I have always been underestimated even when I've proven myself to have a balanced viewpoint in most aspects of life. My reference coded name between some members of my entourage is "Petit Taximan a Londres" which I have no problem with because it's not a crime to be a taxi driver. With my taxi driving career, I've given my children solid ground to stand on from which to build a better career than mine. I might not be the perfect father that they wish for, but at least they will not be starting from where I did. If they end up a taxi driver like their father, they will consider it below their standards. Their upbringing has been a million miles away from their parents'. If they become taxi drivers as a substitute to their intended career, they'll be considered below standard having been brought up in a country full of opportunities. I have learned to listen and that was a difficult thing to do at first, but it is the most intelligent thing and a very important way to learn. I was conditioned to practise being quiet because whenever I started a conversation with my rider, nine out of ten times the rider was not interested. However, when my rider has something to discuss or even an experience to share, they expect me to contribute. Listening far outweighs speaking. Every time I've had the privilege of driving a rider with a visual impairment, they are always alert to sounds coming from within and outside my cab. Meanwhile, I've taken many riders with hearing impairments and the comparison of both disabilities is so different. Whenever I picked up a rider with a hearing impairment, we usually had limited conversation because they rely on the movement of my lips to interpret what I am saying. It's also very problematic when they are in the back seat. Most riders with visual impairments are noticeable with their guide dogs and I've always had a lot to discuss with them. I temporarily forget about their disabilities until the presence of their guide dog reminds me of their condition. I listen to every rider in my cab, even those who are quiet, and it has helped shape the person I am today. During my driving career, I've listened and shared thoughts with people from all walks of life. I've listened to more conversations than this book can handle and that knowledge would be hard to find in other professions.

Through the account service that Ruskin Cars had with King's College Hospital, Guy's and Saint Thomas' Hospital, I was exposed to the way the British medical system operates. Our duties included the transportation of medical staff from one hospital to another. During trips, they often shared experience that I could not have received if not for my job. I picked up a consultant on a Saturday morning from King's College Hospital to Cromwell Hospital which is a private hospital. During the trip, he explained the situation of the patient he went to see on his day off because the duty doctor needed some urgent decision. The patient was a twenty-five year old who, at that young age, had destroyed his liver through excessive alcohol consumption. He told me the only way out was through a liver transplant. Being young, the patient was prioritised for a match but his historical alcohol abuse was a major dilemma in deciding whether he could be given a second chance. I could see that the consultant was stressed and really wanted to help that young man rebuild his life. It reminded me of the young people I usually drive on a Saturday night who were already drunk and on their way to nightclubs. My rider specialised in transplants. He told me the amount of alcoholics in the country is a major concern. Britain has got a culture that celebrates every event with alcohol. I've lost a close member of my family through alcohol abuse back in Cameroon. He had cirrhosis but all the doctors could do was to drain water from his liver until he passed away. Towards the end of his days on earth, he told me some people were trying to kill him. I asked him who those people were, but he couldn't say. I knew he was dying because of his dependency on alcohol for many years. My job experience had already given a rear-view mirror of the problem that, in my hometown, could be associated with witchcraft. I grew up with the knowledge that my father's death wasn't natural. I was told time and time again that he died because of some traditional instructions that he disobeyed. When I arrived in the United Kingdom, upon registering with my general practitioner, I was asked on the form if I had stroke, diabetes or blood pressure problems in my family. My father had a stroke and was paralysed for a long time before he passed away. At the time, I don't think the doctor treating him knew what he was suffering from, let alone knew what to do with his condition. It may seem a long while but many people still adhere to that theory. They are in a corridor with the witchcraft on the left and the religious exorcist preacher on the right.

There was a regular rider who used my service and relied on me for the transportation of her mother. I took her when she needed to attend a hospital appointment due to her advanced age. Her mother lived on a big council estate near our office. On that particular day, everyone knew that the gas supply was going to be suspended for the day due to building work. With no heating in her flat, this was a problem for the old lady. I was booked to pick her up from her house and take her to her daughter's house to spend the day in the warm environment there. By then, I'd known her mother for a while. Despite her advanced age, she remembered many stories and usually narrated them to me while on a trip. Originally from Senegal, it meant that our conversations were carried out in French and she always remembered what we'd spoken about before. During the trip that morning, which was under a mile but in the rush-hour traffic jam, we had a constructive discussion. When I arrived at her daughter's address, I called her to send someone down to help her mother with the little luggage that she had. In the meantime, she got out of my cab and shut the door; she was very independent, even with her advanced age. I got out of my cab as well and walked towards the rear to remove her luggage.

'Just wait there, Maa, your grandson is coming down to help you,' I told her.

I expected her to call the boy's name for reassurance, but she didn't. I realised she was not responding to what I was saying. I walked towards her and saw that she was leaning on the cab with her eyes open but not moving. I sensed danger. I held her hands and called her name. She couldn't speak and was only standing because I was keeping her upright. I knew straight away she was having a heart attack. My experience of working at the hospital equipped me to know how the condition manifested. However, practically, I didn't know what to do at that critical moment. An intervention from an off-duty doctor came at a pivotal moment. He took her from me, laid her on the floor, performed CPR on her and asked me to call the emergency services. I knew he was a doctor because he asked them for a specific service. The ambulance staff came with the right equipment which was brought by emergency motorbike service. When I visited her at the hospital, I asked her if she remembered me. She told me everything that happened until she got out of my cab, and then she woke up in her hospital bed. The scene that I witnessed that day was one of the reasons I believed I'd learned a lot from when I began my driving career. Everything happened in front of me and was my responsibility. Although I was a novice to the situation at the beginning, at the end I was more knowledgeable. Having been exposed to the many medical conditions of patients attending hospital, I was aware of the struggle that health poses in our daily lives. I knew there were no demons in my rider as I was comfortable with her when she was healthily strong. I was mentally prepared that heart attack, stroke and high blood pressure can affect anyone, any time, anywhere.

Transporting patients and medical professionals on account from Maudsley Hospital to Bethlem Royal hospital in Beckenham was a fascinating learning experience on mental health. When a job was allocated to me from the Maudsley Hospital, I never knew what type of rider I was going to be transporting. It wasn't until the rider was in my cab and we were heading to their destination that I'd know who they were. There were two types of riders on that account job: the patient and the medical staff, both of whom would present different behaviours and both to me were educational. I picked up a psychiatrist who had just returned from his holiday break.

'I'm happy to return to work. I had some quality time in South Africa. Nice weather, good food, lots of places to visit … but it was time to return,' he told me.

'How long were you there for?' I asked him.

'Three months,' he replied.

'Wow! That was a long break,' I said.

'I needed that time away from here … but it's time to get back to my patients. They drive me up the wall sometimes, but they are good people with their own personal, touching stories,' he said.

'Listening to someone's story can create an emotional reaction, can't it?' I said.

'That's why I'm doing everything for my patients to get back to normality,' he replied.

I also picked up a patient talking continuously to himself throughout the whole trip. At first, I thought he was talking to me but then realised he was thinking out loud. He was not conscious that he was voicing his thoughts and that was the thing that made me realise that he was a patient. At no time did I feel threatened during the trip. In 1995, shortly after I arrived in London, I bought my first mobile phone. I was engaged in a phone conversation near Brixton station. One of my relatives saw me and thought that I was talking to myself; she concluded that I was mad. When I phoned my extended family back home, they asked me if I was feeling better. They had heard I was mentally unstable, that I had been spotted talking to myself on a popular high street. However, through our conversation they could tell that I sounded stable and I was reasoning in a sane manner and were very relieved. I remembered using my phone on hands-free with my handset in my pocket. I kept my handset in my pocket for protection and during the conversation, I was making a lot of hand movements. At the time, a lot of people were using Walkmans to listen to their favourite music when they were on the move. There were some users who used them to practise their a cappella and dance routines. I was never known for having any ambitions in the music department, leaving my relative to believe I was talking to myself. I grew up with the experience of seeing families keeping their loved one chained in a spare room or cellar when they became mentally unstable. They didn't want their loved one to be strolling the streets with dirty clothes and talking to themselves. Mental disorder was a taboo subject in society back home.

As a little boy, I witnessed a neighbour whom I had known from birth who lived with chains on his hands and feet from the time he became mentally unstable until he passed away. That dark period of what I witnessed has never been erased from my memory. The only treatment he received was from a witch doctor who, from analysing his approach to the patient that he was supposed to help, needed help himself. He was inflicting violence on someone who needed help from a condition that can affect every human being on this planet. He was classified as a mad person in our society and that stigma was degrading. Because of his popularity, my friends and I were regularly around him when the witch doctor came to treat him. I could see the frailty in his eyes. The witch doctor had a very unusual bunch of long brooms that he used to whip the poor man on the same spot continuously. He believed he could beat him back to sanity. Today, the people of my country have shifted the responsibilities of the treatment of mental health disorder patients to religious exorcist preachers. The charlatan witch doctors based their theories on casting out demons from the vulnerable which is an abstract from ancient Catholicism. People actually believe that a human being who is out of sync with their mind, body and soul is the result of a demon who has miraculously gained access into their body. My job has given me the privilege of transporting an outpatient from a mental health department. During our trip, he told me how he had his life back after going through the most difficult period of his life. Although he had lost everything, through the help of his psychiatrist, he was slowly getting back to normal. The lack of information in a naïve African population has created a vacuum for opportunists, religious and witchcraft self-appointed gurus to capitalise on some of the public.

Living with my uncle for two years in a remote area, was a life-changing experience for me. It was a seven mile walk to the main tarred road where public transport vehicles could be found. My uncle was one of the biggest traditional herbalists in the vicinity and I witnessed many people with illnesses get help. He knew different herbal remedies to treat various conditions, but he never pretended to be a witch doctor. Whenever a patient visited him with a problem, he usually examined her/him with questions and then he would check their eyes, tongue and urine. His son, who was a bit older than me, would be sent into the jungle to find specific herbs. I usually went with him because there was little to do in the village. I learned how intelligent my cousin was as he knew the exact herbs needed. During my time in my village, I saw many patients who came with serious illnesses and left in a far better healthy condition. The most common visitors were women with fertility problems and most of them also got the result they longed for. One day, while I was in the jungle with my uncle, I found the courage to ask him where he had learned his abundant knowledge of the herbal field. My uncle was an influential man who was not used to young people asking him questions. He was a man of his time but my town-boy courage was my driving force. He was much older than my mother and the next of kin of my grandfather. Surprisingly, he used that opportunity to describe the life of his father who I hadn't had the luxury of knowing.

'Everything that I know about the treatment of human beings came from your grandfather. I was never too lazy to go into the jungle to fetch herbs whenever I was sent,' he told me.

My uncle seized every opportunity to turn me into a smart boy; he wanted me to have a can-do attitude.

'Where did he get the knowledge from?' I asked him. He smiled.

'I never had the courage to ask him those sorts of questions,' he replied.

My uncle knew I was naïve to my traditions and needed help to understand my family tree.

'Your grandfather was very influential in this entire area, not only from his herbal knowledge but also from his physical appearance,' he continued.

He knew I'd eventually return to my township life after primary school as there was no secondary school around.

'What's your name?' he asked me.

'Andrew Njanjo,' I replied.

He shook his head.

'Those are your given names. Your name at conception is Wafeu Nana … my father's name. Although it is not written down in any paper that you'll ever carry, according to our tradition, that's your name,' he said.

From that day, I felt like I was older than my real age. On countless occasions that I was just with him, he used many examples to remind me of my potential.

The knowledge passed on from father to son, and grandsons was done verbally. With the verbal teaching and by taking his son to the jungle while on duty, much information was lost. I guessed my uncle was trying to tell me that his father was ten times a better herbalist than him. I didn't have the courage at the time to ask him why my grandfather didn't write all that he knew down. His descendants could have benefited greatly from his knowledge rather than just verbally teaching them. Twenty years since my uncle passed away, and the change on the villagers' health can be noticed by the decline of their well-being. The overreliance on western medicine, which they struggled with the affordability of, has put a strain on their health. My cousin, who learned the practice of using herbal medicine from his father, has moved to the city. What he knows is also ten times less than his father and gradually the knowledge is diminishing through the generations. Driving around London, the capital city of a country which boasts of its free market policy, there is not an area where a Chinese medicine shop can't be found and they are delighted with their return because their service is in demand. I accepted a request to pick up a rider from a Chinese health shop. He was going to another Chinese shop at Chinatown, central London and back. During our time spent in the traffic jam, we were having a conversation and I seized the opportunity to ask him about their practice.

'When it states on a Chinese health shop that there is a doctor ... is it just someone with herbal knowledge or someone with a PHD in medicine?' I asked him.

'The owners of those shops are qualified medical doctors with a PHD from a Chinese university,' he replied.

'Wow! I didn't know that ... that's real knowledge shared,' I said.

I thought my grandfather's generation did a disservice to the future of African ancient herbal treatment. They did not create a structure in which knowledge could be shared between Africans who are interested in healthcare. The effects can be noticed by the African reliance on miracles through religion and fortune tellers because their natural gift has been lost somehow.

SEVENTEEN

PROSPERITY GOSPEL

It was a Sunday morning – few drivers worked during that period – but I accepted a request from an address I was familiar with. The rider was of African descent from Nigeria. I knew she always went to the same church on a Sunday. Many riders liked my service because I didn't judge or criticise what they chose to do. My sole reason for transporting people was to get paid at the end of it. When someone got used to me after several trips, they would start to speak to me on a personal and emotional level. On that Sunday morning, when I arrived at my rider's address, her husband and children were not with her.

'I'm on my own today with a lot of coolers. I hope they will fit in your car,' my rider said.

'Wow! That's a lot of food you've got there,' I responded.

I was taking her to a different location from her usual Sunday mass.

'You're not going to church today?' I asked.

'It's a church but not the one you know,' she replied. 'This one is an event … a big gathering.'

She didn't know the area well but she told me she had been there before. I checked my map and estimated that the trip would take about an hour and a half.

'It's a large warehouse that has been converted for a big church event. When we reach the area, I'll know where to go,' she told me.

I loaded the coolers into my multi-purpose vehicle, and my rider sat in the front seat.

When I had driven her previously, with her family, she always had a conversation with her husband. Alone that day, it seemed she had a lot to discuss.

'I have not slept all night. I'm feeling it right now,' she told me.

She wound her window down to get some fresh air.

'It must be an interesting gathering for you to miss your Sunday mass for it,' I said.

'It's a miraculous gathering, with ministers coming from around the world. Even my preacher is there,' she told me.

I noticed she was struggling to stay awake. She gave me a leaflet of the event that had a collage of many church minsters on it. All were men except for two women who were guest speakers.

'Will you come to this gathering as my guest?' she asked me.

I didn't answer her question about attending her once in a lifetime event. It was a long drive and I didn't want to create any awkwardness.

'Do you believe in Jesus Christ?' she asked me.

I realised she wasn't going to talk about anything else.

'No!' I replied.

'I guess you are not a Christian,' she said.

'Your guess is spot on. I'm not a Christian,' I replied.

'Are you a Muslim?' she asked.

'My first name is Andrew. Even my parents were not Muslim. Neither am I,' I replied.

'What religion are you then?' she asked.

'I'm a Pan-African?' I told her.

'What is Pan-African,' she asked.

'It is the common interest that Africans share whatever their geographical position in the world,' I told her.

'What does that mean? What common interest? I'm African but with a different culture from, say, someone in Somalia,' she told me.

'Solidarity between the African born and diaspora Africans. They are together in the liberation struggle,' I told her.

'That's not a religion. As an African, you're either Christian or Muslim and nothing stops you being a Pan-African at the same time,' she said.

'Christianity and Islam began as a movement but were turned into commercial organisations. Pan-Africanism is a non-profit organisation,' I told her.

My rider was well informed and was very friendly in her arguments. I've transported many Christians who are blinded by their strong stance on their beliefs.

'I have a lot of respect for Christians but not for the organisation. They have turned it into a commercial entity … selling hopes that can only be realised when you're dead. Pan-Africanism connects me with real people who have affected and shaped the life we're actually living. It gives me a platform to build a realistic life,' I told her.

That Sunday morning, I drove from south-east London to Dover near the ferry. With a traffic jam, the trip took an hour and a half.

'Do you believe in a superpower?' she asked me.

'It depends … in my traditional language, we call our ancestors FEUSIH, meaning laying God,' I replied.

'That's a tradition widely practised in ancient Africa … Andrew, do you believe in God, the almighty?' she asked me.

I thought she wanted a cab for crying out loud.

'You are asking me about the philosophy of the European belief system. The scripture is based on European ancestral history. I'm African,' I replied.

She was still not satisfied with my world view. She was obsessed with Jesus.

'Before Christianity, Africans were living on this planet. They had their belief system which was interrupted by foreign invasion,' I told her.

'Have you ever been touched by the holy ghost?' she asked me.

'Ghost?' I asked.

She nodded.

'Never!' I replied.

'What I mean is, have you ever been in a difficult position where you couldn't find a solution? Then a solution miraculously resolved it,' she asked me.

'Nope!' I replied.

'I have, and that's why my belief is as strong as a rock,' she said.

'I've never had any difficulties in my entire life … only obstacles … and I never worried about obstacles because they are what keep me going. Without obstacles I do not have a challenge and without challenges I don't learn and I can't strive … that spirit I inherited from my ancestors,' I told her.

She looked confused.

'Can I pray with you?' she asked me.

Her proposal sounded amusing. All I wanted to do was to drive her to her destination safely.

'Go on, let's pray,' I said.

I was being sarcastic but she didn't realise. My riders are my clients and they are my priority. I like to leave them with a pleasant memory. In my mind, I was wondering how someone could be so courageous as to ask a cab driver if he needs to pray. I'm out to earn a living not to seek spiritual ascent. She was silently meditating for two minutes and then started to pray. Jesus was in every sentence of her prayer. In a short moment, she freed me from all my sins. She then authorised utterances from the Holy Ghost. In the space of five minutes, I was in total deliverance in the name of the Holy Ghost. She invoked God by asking him to vomit fire seven times. She then opened her hand and threw it towards me with a powerful voice. 'RECEIVE IT,' she said. I thought the scene was over but no, after thirty seconds, she began speaking in tongues. It was a language I don't think even she understood. I waited for five minutes to make sure the prayer was over.

'What was the meaning of that last bit?' I asked her.

'At that moment, I was connected to the Holy Spirit,' she replied.

This performance was better than I'd ever seen in a theatre. If she auditioned like that in front of any Hollywood film director, she would definitely get a second call. She was very passionate and emotional, she was in the moment and melted into the character. She wasn't acting, she was playing the role; the entire scene was in sync, unedited and uninterrupted. I suspended my disbelief and was in the moment with her, just like I often do when watching a film. I thanked her for taking me into her inner thoughts. Whatever our differences in beliefs, the intention was priceless. Moments after that scene we arrived at her destination. She was slowly coming out of her meditating mood.

'Think about life after this material-driven world we temporarily inherit,' she told me.

'I will. Right now, there are many obstacles in front of me to overcome. When the time is right, I'll join you,' I told her.

She was still ignorant of my sarcastic remarks.

'My brother, the time is now,' she replied.

She looked at me with a serious expression.

'I hear you, but you know I have to get back to work,' I told her.

I offloaded her food coolers from my cab, got my fare and returned to the cab office.

On the way back, I was happy because my goal had been achieved. I was paid the right amount for the trip and that's the end result I aimed for. When I left the shores of my homeland, Cameroon, finding a place in heaven was never in the list of my goals. God, Jesus and his disciples, angels, the holy spirit and Lucifer are preached about everywhere in Africa. I felt rather sorry for my rider who, I assumed, had come here as a migrant to search for a better life, conscious of being in bondage from birth and trapped in post-colonial dogma. However, I knew there was nothing I could do even though I'm part of the organisation that has always been on a journey to effect change. I've been living with the syndrome caused by the darkest moments in the history of mankind. Using guns and Bibles to physically frighten and paralyse African minds has been perpetual. It will never change as long as people like my rider keep feeding their generation with ignorant teachings. I travelled to the UK to gain financial freedom and give my family the opportunities I never had. All I wanted was education, healthcare, justice, human rights protection and the opportunity to build a prosperous future. She believes I should not worry about this material world and instead, I should focus on the life after death. This is the biggest misconception I've ever heard. Financial freedom was the only thing that was absent in my life while growing up in Cameroon. The entirety of sub-Saharan Africa has adopted capitalism and that has rendered many families in dire straits. When I'm dead, I'll think about that phase of life but for now, I've got the imminent struggle of elevating myself with the opportunities I've got in front of me. We're so enslaved by our emotions that reality becomes absent in our thought process. We hold dear to meaningful things that have no effect in our struggle.

There are many new African entrepreneurs in Europe and America who are capitalising on the weaknesses and struggles that migrants encounter. They are using theological teaching to target people in difficulty who haven't got the capacity to find solutions to their woes. The geographic location is an obstacle for many of us who migrated in the diaspora. It's difficult to understand but we are like children who are learning about life around us. Pan-African preachers like Doctor Martin Luther King used their platform to fight for the equality of African people without benefiting financially. These new entrepreneurs use their platform to become rich. Unlike conventional Catholic ways of preaching, these rich entrepreneurs spread fear to their congregations and keep them anxious. The followers of these mega churches are just modern slaves. They don't know that they are mentally enslaved. The food that my rider was talking to this mega event was a donation and she still had to pay her tithe, in addition to the cab fare. The amount of money contributed to these entrepreneurs in their churches can go a long way in Africa to help a lot of disadvantaged children out of poverty.

When I arrived in the UK, I met a young woman who was also from my hometown. We became good friends and got on so well that we started to fancy each other. The relationship had everything except the final bit, the icing on the cake. She wanted me to attend her church and become a member before our relationship could be completed. I wanted to do everything to please her, regardless of my resentment to the religious teaching. It was my only opportunity to secure that relationship so I decided to attend her church. The pastor was one of the best actors in that field. During the service, I wanted to donate a pound; she refused and insisted I gave more. After several arguments, I finally surrendered and donated my five hard-earned pounds. I was cleaning toilets and watching staircases for a living; understandably, I was reluctant to let go of my money easily. I thought I had satisfied her needs and had now secured the relationship, but there was still one more test. The preacher announced that anyone who was new should raise their hand. I didn't; she asked me to.

'I will not be coming back. What's the point?' I asked her. She insisted.

In my mind, it seemed I must raise my hand or lose everything. I raised my hand and was taken to a separate chamber with about twenty others. I knew there were other junior actors about pretending to be newcomers. What they were doing reminded me of my Sunday School days when I was a child and adults were trying to groom us. At the end of the meeting, the group leader told us that we were all going to pray. At the end of the prayer, she started to speak in tongues, and most people joined in. I was looking at them as if they had some mental disorder. I couldn't believe what I was witnessing. One was crying. My body was in that room but my mind was long out of there.

After church, I explained to my friend what had happened to us in that chamber. I was surprised when she laughed and reassured me that I'd nothing to worry about.

'It was the right of passage ... a new beginning of becoming a born-again,' she told me.

That was the first time I'd heard the term 'born again' as a segregated group of Christians.

'Do you pray in tongues?' I asked her.

'It comes naturally when I am connected,' she replied.

'Which language is that?' I asked her. 'I didn't understand the meaning of the words.'

'You don't need to, Andrew. It comes and goes before you know it,' she replied.

We often argued about all kinds of things but still stayed good friends. We were similar ages, had the same background and were fluent in our language which was the pidgin English widely spoken in the southwest of Cameroon. However, our religious views were miles apart. I knew she had attended Christ The King College Tiko, a renowned Catholic institution. Being born again and praying in a language she did not understand was way beyond madness. Our relationship started to misfire; there was an invisible barrier between us. Being enslaved and conned by the people who came to Europe in search for a better life like me was not something I could allow to happen to me wittingly or unwittingly. Our religious differences put our friendship under great stress.

'If you want an intimate relationship with me, you must become a born-again Christian,' she told me.

I was lucky to have lived with my uncle who guided me to my roots. I was not ready to throw away the two years of training for a relationship that was not guaranteed to last. It also meant that my mother and father would become a shadow in my life; they would serve no purpose to me since I would be born again. My mind is the driving force of my body, and my body will always follow my mind unquestionably. I was not prepared to be released from my reality and ancestral roots, and start to live in a land created and controlled by the new religious entrepreneurs.

When I walked into the church, it was like a performing arts theatre. It looked nothing like the usual Catholic and Presbyterian churches I was accustomed to. On that day, I was greeted by many people around the premises of the church and I just thought they were friendly. During the service, I realised why I was dressed the same as the church's orchestra. I was wearing a red jacket with blue navy trousers which was identical to the musicians. The three-hour service seemed like thirty minutes because of the abundance of activities and the vibrant atmosphere. The minister himself was, to my mind, a very entertaining narrator. The orchestra was in synchronisation with every break during the sermon, eliminating boring gaps that are common in Catholic churches. Some native Africans have got undiagnosed emotional disorder syndrome, including myself. I was emotionally glued to the sermon rather than ingesting and digesting the quality of the preaching. Unlike most of the congregation who were mainly native Africans, I knew I was temporarily suspending my disbelief because the atmosphere was akin to a scripted and well-rehearsed performance. There were cameras in the church, set at different angles to record the events. After the service, they were selling the DVD that had been edited and put together. When my friend watched it, it had an even more believable feel than actually being part of the congregation. The different cameras angles showed the action and reaction of the preacher and the audience which she was part of but could not see. In the pre-social media era, the only thing available to keep the memory of the special event was her DVD. She played that DVD many times during the week which meant that she was unwittingly hooked on the preaching style of her church.

I concluded that it was the born-again preacher's way of entrapping their congregation. The sermon was about faith; the priest questioned the strength of the congregation's faith. He said Jesus and his disciples were travelling to America from London in a passenger aircraft. I was lost at the beginning of the sermon because according to the scripture, when Jesus was on earth, aircraft were not invented yet. He continued. They were cruising at thirty-two-thousand feet and Jesus was sleeping in the first-class cabin. The disciples were in business class. I felt like there was a little exaggeration about that because classism is a modern concept, and Jesus was not wealthy. He continued. All of a sudden, the aircraft started descending rapidly. Jesus' disciples started to pray but the pilot could not stabilise the plane. The disciples started to see mountains, meaning they were going to crash. They rushed to the first-class cabin and found Jesus deep in his sleep. They woke him up in a panicked state; he answered, woke up and witnessed the scene. 'We know if this plane crashes, nothing will happen to you. Please command this aircraft to gain altitude and save us from dying,' said one of his disciples. Jesus laughed. He looked at them, one after another. 'Men of little faith,' he told them. He then commanded the aircraft back to its stable position. The congregation was quiet, just like in a theatre when the performance is very good. The priest looked at them and asked them, 'How strong is your faith?' Everyone sighed to release the tension the performance had caused. Whenever an African is given a script, they turn it into their own words and give the director a mind-blowing performance. That day, I understood why most Africans cast aside their conventional Catholic indoctrination for the newly arrived, born-again performing theatre.

Becoming a servant of and contributor to the fortune of these rich entrepreneurs was out of my psyche. They live a life of luxury I could only dream of just by selling tickets for a ghost space shuttle to their followers. I was not prepared to pay these entrepreneurs to read me bedtime-stories. There's no point organising the next life when I'm unable to effect changes in the present one. There seems to be a hangover of religious beliefs which have derailed African cultures throughout history. The Africans dependency on religious miracles is a conscious double jeopardy. Africans continued to be enslaved throughout the colonial period, waiting for miracles, while other continents were advancing with technology. I had two colleagues who were first-generation African migrants. They migrated to Britain to build a future for themselves and their offspring, just like me. Having the same goal meant we were closer and shared our experiences. Both of them, however, were born-again Christians who never failed to attend their place of worship on a Sunday. Whenever I decided to work on a Sunday, I was left without my usual companions. One of them, without fail, would write down every job and the amount he was paid in his diary.

'Why are you writing down every trip and the amount?' I asked him.

'It's so I can be accurate about the amount of tithe I'm due to pay,' he replied. 'Is it compulsory?' I asked. At the time, I was struggling to pay my tax at the end of the year.

'It's not … I do it to thank God for the energy he gives me throughout the week,' he replied.

'If you earn, say, five hundred pounds during the week, how much will that cost you?' I asked.

'Fifty pounds,' he replied without hesitation.

'Wow! And you still have to declare your tax at the end of the year?' I asked him.

'Taxes are for the country … tithe is spiritual,' he replied.

The cash-in-hand nature of being self-employed is a challenge at the end of the tax year. The thought of giving away ten percent of my gross earnings was mind blowing.

'You're building the fortune of one of the richest public speakers of false promises,' I told him.

Somehow, he was never angry at me.

'You cannot understand until you're touched by the Holy Ghost,' he told me.

'I'd rather keep my hard-earned money and go to hell if the only way to enter heaven is to help some individuals live a life of luxury,' I told him.

He laughed.

'Andrew, do you think there's any enjoyment on this planet? Even the very rich have their own struggle,' he said.

My other colleague was more discreet about his contribution to his church.

'Do you pay tithe in your church?' I asked him.

'That information is between me and my God,' he replied.

He knew I was very vocal about my view on the unsolicited disposal of one's hard-earned money. One day, he told me he had been anointed as a junior preacher in his church by God.

'Why didn't God anoint you to the position of a medical doctor?' I asked him. He went quiet when he realised he was talking to the wrong person. Knowing that I was never going to be silent about the topic, he continued.

'God works in mysterious ways,' he told me.

'Does your priest have a job? Apart from preaching, I mean,' I asked him.

'He doesn't need to have another job, Andrew. He is constantly receiving church goers during the week,' he replied.

'According to the scriptures, even Jesus had a job while he preached the words of his father,' I told him.

'We live in a different era from when Jesus was on earth,' he replied.

'If your priest is a full time church minister, he is living off his congregation,' I told him.

He wasn't happy with my statement.

'The demon is using your personality to do his job,' he said.

'I accept your concept. Christianity has created an invisible monster which their followers can vent their misfortune on,' I replied.

He walked away but somehow our differences of opinion never annoyed him enough to avoid me. My friendship with both drivers continued even though our views were quite opposite. I guess they love to witness the rebel in me on a subject that they hold dearly. Just as it takes a bad scenario to realise the effort someone is putting in to have normality, my colleagues needed a resilient character like me to justify their position. If there is life above the sky and a more comfortable one than the current earth we inhabit, as described by theologians, the super rich with all their wealth would've invested in the most sophisticated technology to relocate there.

A society can only grow if the young are given a platform to develop and explore their potential as I witnessed while growing up. Although poverty is raging in Africa, many people somehow find money to donate to religious institutions but are reluctant to donate to educational institutions. Africa is the only continent which consumes what they don't produce and produces what they don't consume. When I travelled to Britain, one of my jobs was in a primary school. I was a cleaner and I could not believe the level of investment I saw there. I looked back at my primary and secondary school facilities and the comparison was of day and night. It's not a miracle that children in the West grow up with inventive minds and African children are forever relying on miracles. London is one of the richest capital cities in the world with many churches, but they are never full. Europeans are reducing their reliance on the superpowers and focusing more on science. On Sundays, most of the riders who I take to church are black families. Their trips are not to the conventional renowned church buildings but rather, warehouses transformed into places of worship. Driving around London has given me first-hand knowledge of homelessness. I've driven these people many times on a trip and listened to each one of their real human stories. There was a white female who was homeless and was always around our cab office premises as she knew the owner of our cab office. She was always broke because of her generosity towards others who were homeless. Every time she got her social benefit money, she bought drinks for the people who kept her company during her vulnerable moments. One day, she requested a trip and it was my turn on the controller's list. During the trip, she sat in the back of my cab without an alcoholic drink.

'Where're you from?' she asked me.

'I'm from Cameroon,' I replied.

'You speak French, don't you?' she asked. I nodded.

'One side speaks French and the other side speaks English,' I replied.

'If I'm not mistaken,' that's central Africa, isn't it?' she asked.

'How do you know? Have you ever been there?' I asked.

'France has a bigger influence in the central African region than the British,' she replied.

When I arrived at her destination, she gave me a twenty pound note.

'Thank you, driver. Have a good day,' she said.

I thought she had mistaken the twenty pound note for a ten pound one. The trip was in the region of eight to nine pounds maximum.

'Excuse me, please, madam,' I hailed at her.

She turned round, looked at me and came back.

'You forgot your change,' I told her.

'Oh no, don't worry. Keep it. I know you guys are really struggling with all the expenses of running your cabs,' she told me.

When I returned to the cab office, I explained what had happened to the owner of our cab office. He gave me her brief history.

'She was one of the first women I've known who was driven in a Bentley. Her husband was a very wealthy man who was driven in a Rolls Royce. She has always been a devoted Christian. She goes to church at least three times every week. Where you dropped her was near a church, wasn't it?' he asked me. I nodded. 'After her husband's sudden death, she did not organise and protect their wealth legally. Their employees exploited their wealth and ran their company into bankruptcy. That's how she became homeless,' he told me.

I learned how my rider spent three days each week in the church but at night she had nowhere to sleep. Theology teaches Christians to invest in the institution but is not there when they are in need. My rider was homeless and sleeping rough when the church building was empty at night. Donating to religious institutions is a selfish act because the donors are buying their imaginary seat in the sky. My colleagues who filled the pockets of religious actors were far from being generous; they were just pre-booking their seat in the illusive heaven.

During a trip with a rider on a Friday afternoon, there was a debate on LBC radio. The argument was about Muslim women and their style of dress. The presenter was specifically moving the conversation towards face coverings. It was after the French government banned face coverings in public places. He enticed his callers to share their views on whether the women were forced to cover their faces or whether they wore them willingly. My rider was a Muslim woman. I knew that because of her dress choice and she was wearing a hijab. Her accent indicated that she was brought up in Britain but was of Middle Eastern descent. There were many white callers who believe those women had no choice but to adhere to what their men wanted. The majority of Muslim women who called said they wore their face covering because it was something their mother did. I was reluctant to say anything because the topic was very personal to my rider. Out of the blue, a fine voice came out of her covered face. 'No Muslim woman is forced to wear a face covering. It is a personal choice. My dad never spoke to me about covering myself up. I made the decision to please Allah and not a man,' my rider told me.

'For some, it's a personal choice but there are many women who are forced to cover up,' I replied.

'That's what the media always present as reality … it's not true,' she said. 'There are some Islamic countries with jihadi police officers who are going around arresting women who are not covered. That demonstrates that those women have no freedom,' I replied.

'There are different ways to effect change. Some Muslim women uncovered themselves to protest ... to make a statement against what they disagreed with. Trust me, the wearing of a face cover is a personal choice,' she said.

'With respect madam. You can't speak for every Muslim woman,' I replied. Cameroon has got a thirty percent Muslim population living peacefully with a majority of Christians. I grew up seeing Muslim women wearing hijab just like Christian women attending church. However, the niqab, and more so the burqa, was never the dress choice of the female followers of Islam. Although my rider was very polite during our exchanges, she stopped short of agreeing with me on the subject. Three hours after that job, the cab office informed me that an allegation of Islamophobia had been made against me. I grew up in a country with a Muslim president. Both Christian and Muslim holy days were officially declared bank holidays and we celebrated together. I don't have the tendency to be an Islamophobe even though I don't hold religion in high regard. Our cab office had many drivers from the west-African country of Sierra Leone. They were mostly followers of the religion of Islam and somehow their attitudes towards their beliefs were very modest. During our time together at the cab office, they never showed strong emotions towards their religion compared to the born-again Christian drivers. The only period of the year that their religion was noticeable was during Ramadan when throughout the day they were fasting. I was very respectful to them because of my non-intrusive beliefs attitude.

EIGHTEEN

AFRICA, A NEW POLITICAL DIRECTION AWAITS

London attracts many people from all walks of life and living in both continents has given me an interesting view on politicians from the African continent. I picked up a white South African born and bred gentleman from the airport one morning. He now lives and works in Britain but still has parents, siblings and friends in South Africa and was very vocal with his opinions on life and politics there. I didn't interrupt when he was giving me his opinion but afterwards I told him I was not a fan of the political view of the ANC. My resentment about their policy was because the party had been capitalising on the popularity of Nelson Mandela and had taken voters for granted.

'I'm still in contact with my nanny after all these years. She's a black woman who looked after me from birth until I went to university. She's a very nice woman. Every time I travel home, I give her money to look after her kids. During our last meeting, she told me she preferred things when the National Party ruled rather than this present ANC. Things were far better then,' he told me.

I wanted to tell him that charity had never lifted anyone out of poverty but I restrained myself just to allow his contribution to be unedited.

'ANC leaders are not interested in giving opportunity to the young. They're busy filling their bank accounts ... and arguing about the line of succession,' he continued.

I agreed fully with the second point. However, what he didn't say was that the economy of the country was still in the hands of a very few white minorities. Also, the delay of land reform is part of the reason why the majority of the population are still in poverty. When a native African is happy being a nanny all her life to a white family in Africa, it paints the picture of the pathetic conditions that colonialism has created. The political system everywhere in the continent of Africa is based on the ideology of white plutocrats. My first introduction to politics was the anti-apartheid struggle in South Africa. The first ever political activist whom I was singing before I had the opportunity to know what she stood for was Winnie Madikizela-Mandela. When my rider told me about the relationship and conversation he had had with his minder, I understood why Winnie Mandela had spent her entire life fighting injustice inflicted on her patriots. The chances for a basic education were not afforded to the black community and have reduced the nanny to accepting her substandard position. Meanwhile, the child she was babysitting enjoyed an education that gave him the opportunity to find employment in the United Kingdom when things were not fruitful in his native South Africa.

In other African countries, including Cameroon, whose educational system was not segregated and underfunded, the vast majority of the population are educated. Apartheid was the only foreign news from South Africa with images of children my age fighting to survive. When the country finally had a black president, many of we Africans were hoping that those marginalised children would have better living conditions. Minister Louis Farrakhan visited South Africa for a political meeting. In one of his speeches afterwards, he said, 'When my plane landed, at the airport, I saw a black man in chains and the man did not say a word. When I arrived at my hotel, the same man was there, still wrapped in chains. I approached the man and the man told me, "Nothing has changed ... we're still enslaved". When Minister Farrakhan met Winnie Mandela afterwards for their scheduled meeting, he raised the subject. '"My husband couldn't fulfil the promise he made to his people because the whites did not fulfil the promise they made to him," Winnie Mandela told him.

In a proper democracy, a president cannot rely on the promise of a tiny minority to govern the entire country. Nelson Mandela was not elected just because he spent twenty-seven years in prison. He was voted in to implement his manifesto. The ANC won the battle but lost the war. They are in control of the political sector of the country but the economy is still in the hands of the white minorities. My rider's nanny must have been telling him about her political preference out of frustration. No marginalised person can succeed in their quest to replace an oppressed regime and then prefer the system they helped topple.

In the Republic of South Africa, there's only one politician whose rhetoric unifies the entire sub-saharan Africa. Julius Malema MP, the leader of the Economic Freedom Fighters, is the only elected Member of Parliament who truly represents his people. In the South African parliament, there are black MPs who see Julius Malema as a nuisance because he only wants to free his constituency trapped in economic deprivation for decades. The ANC, who have been in control of the political leadership there since Nelson Mandela was released from prison, have had only an empty succession of leaders with vague rhetoric. In one of the few democracies in Africa, Julius Malema is the politician who is being interrogated by the Western media more than any other member of parliament. The political elites are ninety percent black, including the president, but if the economy remains in the hands of the minority whites, blacks will continue to live in deprivation on their home soil. I'm not naïve to the many career politicians who have risen to prominent positions and then settled for the status quo at the demise of their followers. Politicians are historically known for chasing voters and on doing so, try to speak for everyone. Julius Malema is a politician and I know every politician has their flaws, however striking their political viewpoints are. If the land reform happens in South Africa, we might yet again see the same sanctions imposed by the West in Zimbabwe imposed on the South African government. The strongest rhetoric always comes from the politicians in the opposition. When a politician has a slogan that appeals to a growing constituency, they're usually three words. In the case of Julius Malema, it's Economy Freedom Fighter. No politician can give financial freedom to a deprived population. It is up to individuals to capitalise on the system created by the government. Most Africans want to live the artificial lifestyle of the West where everything is on 'buy now and pay later'. The entire continent does not have that facility; what people own is what they can afford. People buy their land and build their homes from scratch, unlike in the West where the bank buys the house for its client. If Julius Malema becomes president one day, it will be a challenge to govern people whose desires are bigger than their abilities. Having been exposed to the Western democratic campaign, I've witnessed the use of these three-word slogans from President Obama with "Yes We Can" and Prime Minister Johnson with "Get Brexit Done". The slogans are inspirational for their followers and help move their campaign forward but impracticable to implement.

When I arrived in Britain, I realised that I had to start from scratch because democracy does not work for the many. The vast majority of the population lives in hope and on artificial wealth. People's reliance on borrowing from their creditors is akin to a medical life-support machine. The Free World, together with the free market, is an entrapment into debt. When I started doing my taxi work in 1996, I knew a regular rider who had a brand new Suzuki Vitara. At the time, I only had my bank card which allowed me to withdraw money at a cash dispensing machine. My rider had about six credit cards including two cash cards. He worked in the ticket kiosk of a London Underground station. Because of limited parking spaces at his workplace, he regularly required my service. At the time, the Suzuki Vitara was the 4x4 of that moment and we all admired him and his little SUV, but he was heavily in debt. He had a salary of about twenty thousand pounds a year and was living in a local government social house. No doubt he could afford to pay for the 4x4 but everything that goes with that flashy lifestyle is expensive. He accumulated credit card debts of over fifty thousand pounds, and that meant he could only afford the minimum payment which meant it took him longer to clear his debt and cost him more than double. That lifestyle was not unique to him. I discovered that most of my riders I was close to due to regularly driving them live that way. The only beneficiaries were the lenders who were shareholders of the rich multinational companies. A capitalist system only benefits those who were born from parents with enough liquidity to help their offspring with an advantaged start. Economic freedom may sound ideal for the majority who are worst off but in practice, no capitalist democratic system can fulfil that dream.

I met a lady who was a registered nurse in Zimbabwe and now practises in a London hospital. After using my service for a long time, we became friends. As a black Zimbabwean, I asked about her political views on the long-term leadership of her country. At the time, Robert Mugabe was one of the oldest presidents in Africa. 'Zimbabweans are proportionally the most educated people compared to other African countries. The leader, whom the West called a dictator, was knighted by the British monarchy when he signed a treaty allowing them thirty years to exploit the land. The land acquired through the colonial invasion had never belonged to the white Zimbabweans. President Mugabe was a friend and ideologue of Nelson Mandela who is their idol today,' she told me.

My rider took a great interest in the political sphere of her country.

'Keeping Nelson Mandela in prison for twenty-seven years was to paralyse the coordinated movement him and his friend, Mugabe, had. They were together when he illegally left his own country,' she continued.

It was like I was in church, listening to the gospel. I didn't get the chance to insert my thoughts.

'Zimbabwe is the breadbasket of the West and not the breadbasket of Africa. The leader's mission was to reform the land back to the rightful owners,' she said.

The African continent is full of dictators, but the West only highlights those who disagree with their political views. Those who are generous with their natural resources to cling on in power are never seen as dictators. Whenever an African leader has a long plan to get rid of colonial ideology in their country, they are quickly pit against their population by the Western media. White plutocrats owned the intellectual property rights of democracy and they oversee the role of the game; any politician who snoozed they lose. President Robert Mugabe tried to play against the big team and he found himself pit against the population he had dedicated his political life to.

Driving people around London has given me the pleasure to meet people from all different parts of the world. I once picked up a woman from the Congo. Because I speak French, we were able to have a serious exchange when I told her I was from Cameroon.

'We were one country before being divided for colonial interest,' she said. 'Where I'm from, there has been an endless war … but not a conventional war as we know it. It's a war to protect the minefield of uranium. I was born in Kambove. There is child enslavement going on in my village and my traditional values are completely destroyed. I don't think I will ever go back to my beloved hometown,' she told me.

'Hope is what keeps us alive. Things might change for the better one day,' I replied.

She putted on a plastic smile.

'It's a place where airplanes land and take off without a runaway … not even a yard of tarmac on the road. That's the risk those people are prepared to take to get the mine out of there without a trace. If they are prepared to make that risky adventure, there's nothing else that they would not do,' she told me.

This justifies why the Congolese government has turned a blind eye to the problem area and concentrated on their quest for power. The population are concentrating on music as their only realistic way out of poverty.

'Would you have preferred for your hometown to be rich in natural resources like it is and hope one day it will benefit the villagers rather than the foreign invaders? Or wish your hometown was originally poor in natural resources and have no potential of any resources that could help develop the area?' I asked her.

'No amount of wealth can replace my ancestral spiritual home. My traditional cultures that should be passed on through generations are completely lost,' she replied.

When a native African is worrying about their cultural and spiritual ancestral bond, they are ignoring the financial attributes. It may not seem a problem to the beneficiary invaders but to the villagers, it's their entire life shred away.

It's good to have a talent that can elevate one out of poverty, just as I have witnessed generations of musical geniuses do from the Congo. It is a complete dream come true to succeed in their chosen career. However, these overnight successes are not the entrepreneurs who create jobs for the young unemployed to benefit from. They build their own lives from their fortune. Their fortune is rather to buy luxury items and to feel superior in front of their peers who have nothing to look forward to except dreaming of becoming a superstar themselves one day. Those who had the lucky break, after galvanising in front of their country's people about their luxurious lifestyle, turned to social media to advertise the content of their garages and the interior design of their living space. Only fools invest in luxury supercars in the continent of Africa. They will depreciate quickly because of the wear and tear the poor condition of the road will have on them. My job as a taxi driver has helped me understand how car manufacturers rely on the petrol heads visiting their forecourts and avail themselves of their products in exchange of their fortunes. I know very well that a vehicle straight out of the forecourt can only depreciate in value and, even when not in use, should always remain insured, especially the supercars. I have friends who are in the same career as me but spend more on luxury items than investing in their future because they are pressured to keep up with their peers. Whenever I'm travelling for a holiday break in Cameroon, the only gifts that satisfy my friends and family are luxury items. Very often, young people who are not in education, training or jobs want the latest portable phone. However, asking me to sponsor the skills that will be beneficial to them throughout their lives is more important. The plutocrats who are the beneficiaries of the mines in the Congo do not spend their fortune on luxury items that they cannot afford; instead, they are investing in industries in their country that many families depend on. Many of them have statues and places of interest named after them due to the generosities that have brought pre-eminent changes in their area. It's a shame to witness the carnage in the Congo ignored by the successors of Patrice Lumumba, one of the renowned leaders in the continent of Africa.

Thomas Sankara downgraded Burkina Faso's prestigious presidential vehicle to a Renault 4 when he took power. During his time in office, he never subscribed to the Western designer suit most African presidents religiously wear in the hottest climate in the world. However, his approach to his leadership made an everlasting impact on many Africans. He enthusiastically engendered positivity in Africans who had a relaxed attitude to life. His can-do mentality was not only reiterated in his speeches but also in his daily duties. His style of governing his country was a lesson to most of us who held him in high regard. He was always criticising the African dependency on foreign consumption and thought we should be consuming what we produced ourselves. He was the only African leader who championed the emancipation of women. In reality, Thomas Sankara was ahead of his time. Even though his reign was very short, no other African leader has been as inspirational as him. When I was a teenager, I mourned the death of Thomas Sankara like I'd known him personally. When the world's media publicly announced that my idol was dead, it brought back the memory of how I felt when I lost my father. I knew it was the end of my hero and I would never hear his positive message again; a man who stood up to the bullying colonialists while telling us, the people he spoke for, to live within our means.

During the arms trade exhibition, I picked up a rider from a luxury hotel in Brentford. He was going to the exhibition at the ExCel centre in East London. My rider had a badge which I believed was his pass to the exhibition as a guest. He was a gentleman from the Middle East I guessed; he spoke very good English with an Arabic accent. We were having a conversation and he started telling me about his weeklong experience in the ExCel centre. He was excited about the modern technological war equipment that was on show.

'My favourite weapon so far has been a robot I was introduced to yesterday. My friend, it can fight a big military troop from thousands of miles away. My friend, it has the capacity to recharge its energy without human contact,' he told me.

I felt that repeatedly finishing his sentence with 'my friend' was a bit patronising. I didn't challenge him about it because I guessed it was normal to address a stranger as a friend in Arabic. I've noticed that with Asian riders who have got into the habit of addressing me as a friend even though we've never met before.

'These drones, are they a force for good?' I asked him.

'My friend, drone technology is so sophisticated that future war conflicts are going to be settled by unmanned systems,' he replied.

He was very excited to tell me about the unbelievable things he had been shown during his weeklong attendance at the warmongering show. What I was listening to was the rich states who, at all costs, are preparing to destroy mankind to protect their vanity. He was undoubtedly the agent of an oil-rich aggressive state who felt so insecure that they needed to exchange their natural resources for something they may never use. During that period, I took many African riders to the arms exhibition show but they were very quiet on the subject. I witnessed people from all walks of life entering the human destructive market show. I thought that if the arms trade was an African company, the Westerners would have referred the shareholders to the International Court of Justice. China, who recently received foreign aid, has turned its economy around to become the creditors to the West and the entire world. African countries, with all their natural resources, need foreign aid like their life depend on it. This money buys the givers a superior status over the receiver. A gift that is conditioned to equip a failed state to avail themselves with military equipment to hang on to power. Thomas Sankara was a military personnel who graduated in the military academy in Madagascar. But during his reign, he used his mental bravery from the military to encourage productivity rather than conflict.

Since I lost my father, I've never replaced the empty space his death left in my life but I've learned to live with it. A few months before he was taken ill, I came back from school one day at around 3 p.m. He was not back from the farm and it was very unusual for him to stay that long. It was raining heavily so I decided to run the two-mile journey to look for him. When I got to the farm, he wasn't there; I knew that because his pipe and lighter were not where he usually kept them. On my way back, my mind was full of thoughts about many things that could've happened to him and if my suspicions were real, what would my future be. When I arrived back home and saw him there, I explained to him what I'd done. He laughed.

'You hardly ever go to the farm willingly. It has taken a situation like this to know the important things in life. Thunderstorms and lightning were what delayed me … but, what I've learned from you, is that, you've got the will to do things but not the need to ignite your desire,' he told me.

My father spoke to me in pidgin English. I was sent to live in my village for two years after his death; it was also his resting place. I used to walk around thinking I would meet him just one last time, even for an hour or two, just to discuss what direction he wanted me to take in the future. My desire never materialised and when Thomas Sankara died, I knew his contributions during his short life were enough for me to build my life around his ideology. Before my father died, he had already created a corridor for me to have plenty of opportunities. Every time I travel around this great city, I see people from different parts of the world and when I'm lucky enough to take them on a ride, it is always a lesson learned through conversations that are different every time. Although I was an orphan and being brought up by just one parent, millions of children with both parents suffer the same fate like me. I'm amongst the lucky ones who have somehow slipped out of the poverty net and built a future for myself and my offspring. Until toothless African leaders change direction and start to lead the continent to benefit Africans rather than foreign plutocrats who have no interest in developing Africa, generations will remain forever entrapped in poverty.

SPECIAL THANKS

Personal thanks to Mr Martin Awah Atanga for being there for me throughout my stay in London. Maggie Dodson who has been a mentor to me from 1996 till date. I will be forever grateful to Mama Lucy Nkwameni for giving me the opportunity to live in London to tell my story. I am blessed with the abundance of love shown by Mama Suzanne Fankham. Mama Odette Yanzè's unconditional love for me has been something I will take to my grave. A friend like Roger Kuébové Pehuie doesn't come very often. You have been my backbone. My wife Alvine whom I consider my biggest critic has helped me in completing this book.